RAISING MONEY FOR ACADEMIC AND RESEARCH LIBRARIES

A How-To-Do-It Manual
for Librarians

Edited by:
BARBARA I. DEWEY

*HOW-TO-DO-IT MANUALS
FOR LIBRARIES*
Number 18

Series Editor: Bill Katz

NEAL-SCHUMAN PUBLISHERS, INC.
New York, London

Published by Neal-Schuman Publishers, Inc.
100 Varick Street
New York, NY 10013

Printed and bound in the United States of America

Library of Congress Cataloging-in-Publication Data

Raising money for academic and research libraries : a how-to-do-it
   manual for librarians / edited by Barbara I. Dewey
      p.   cm. — (How-to-do-it manuals for libraries ; no. 18)
    Includes bibliographical references and index.
    ISBN 1-55570-082-9
    1. Library fund raising—Handbooks, manuals, etc.   2. Libraries,
University and college—Finance—Handbooks, manuals, etc.
3. Research libraries—Finance—Handbooks, manuals, etc.   I. Dewey,
Barbara I.   II. Series.
Z683.R34   1991
025.1′1—dc20   91-40566
                                     CIP

CONTENTS

FOREWORD

I am pleased to write a foreword for *Raising Money for Academic Libraries* because of my strong belief in the public-private partnership for the support of libraries. More than a concept embracing the unique funding structure of the library—where government and the private sector must necessarily come together financially to ensure the continued operation of libraries and library networks—the philosophical roots for this alliance are traceable to Thomas Jefferson's day. The library is a proving ground where "the energies of the individual can be harnessed toward constructive social goals; and where public obligation is melded with personal generosity." I refer readers to the words of Edward Everett, past president of Harvard College, who wrote, "The American way was to make the care of the mind from outset a part of the public economy, the growth of knowledge a portion of its public wealth." Responsibility for the perpetuation of cultural values must by carried by as many forces in American society as possible, all contributing to the common weal.

It is appropriate that librarians and library development professionals, not to mention university presidents and administrators, instruct the public about the riches of the greatest of all intellectual resources found in the nation's libraries. Libraries are as old as civilization. From the clay tablets of Babylonia to the computers of modern research libraries stretch more than 5,000 years of men's and women's insatiable desire to establish written immortality. It is, therefore, critical that colleges and universities across this nation and around the world recognize and promote libraries as worthy recipients of philanthropy. Our intellectual heritage depends on the success of this mission. It cannot be done by a single financial source.

Raising Money for Academic Libraries provides practical and constructive advice for all types of academic and research libraries embarking on comprehensive library development programs. The authors are among the most successful library development specialists in the country and provide readers with a thorough grounding in topics related to fundraising with a specific focus on the academic and research library setting.

Vartan Gregorian
President, Brown University

ACKNOWLEDGMENTS

The editor wishes to thank all past and present members of the Development Officers of Research Academic Libraries (DORAL) group for their commitment and assitance to this project.

INTRODUCTION

by Barbara I. Dewey

The 1990s are proving to be an important decade for academic library development programs. During the 1980s, it seemed that every academic library in the country was either working on some aspect of a development program or was about to embark on one. Now, with many academic libraries facing difficult budget constraints, interest and activity in the development field is even greater.

As the number of academic library development programs has grown, so has the need for related information and resources. In 1987, a small group of library development officers decided to address this need, which they did not believe was being met at the time by existing organizations. Professional fundraising groups, such as the National Society of Fund Raising Executives (NSFRE) and the Council for the Advancement of Secondary Education (CASE), existed, but were not dedicated specifically to libraries. The American Library Association's Library Administration and Management Association (LAMA) had an active section on fundraising focusing on all types of libraries, but it did not attract development professionals. The ALA's Association of College and Research Libraries had not yet begun to address library development within its organization.

The organization this small group of professional library development officers began is now known as DORAL, N.A., Development Officers of Research Academic Libraries, North America. Their first meeting was held in the spring of 1987 at the University of Michigan. Founding members included Joan Hood, University of Illinois at Urbana-Champaign; Linda Bowers, Ohio State University; Deborah Reilly, University of Wisconsin; Susan Jordan, Northwestern University; Betty Smith, University of Michigan; Linda Safran, then at Johns Hopkins University; Mary Bailey Pierce, University of Miami; Chacona Johnson, then of Wayne State University; Sam Streit, Brown University; and Barbara Dewey, University of Iowa. The group, unaffiliated with any organization, has met twice a year since 1987 and consists mainly of persons whose primary job is academic library development for institutions belonging to the Association of Research Libraries (ARL). The majority of DORAL members are development professionals rather than professional librarians.

THE NEED FOR INFORMATION

The need expressed by the formation of this group highlights why academic library fundraising is such a vital activity. These seasoned development officers were not finding information on library development either on their own campuses or in philanthropic associations. In fact, they often found that many people on their campuses, including foundation personnel, campus administrators, and even some library directors, simply did not believe that the library was an attractive magnet for donations or grants. The DORAL members knew this was not the case. Collectively, they were having major success attracting donations, in some cases from individuals and corporations who had never given to their campuses in the past. These new donors were attracted specifically to library projects. It is now clear that external funding opportunities for academic libraries are not only a reality but are a successful way to move the library forward programmatically.

As an early member of DORAL I began to see, after only two meetings, the wealth of expertise and information the members possessed, and I encouraged the group to collaborate on a book devoted solely to academic library development. As a newcomer to the field, I received invaluable information and ideas from my colleagues in DORAL, and I wanted this knowledge made available to others embarking on library development programs. *Raising Money for Academic and Research Libraries: A How-To-Do-It Manual for Librarians* is the result of this effort. It is intended to address some of the most critical topics facing library development professionals, library directors, and university administrators today.

AN OVERVIEW

Why are academic library development program of such growing interest? Library directors, seeing their institutions involved in large campaigns, want the library to be included within the overall institutional fundraising effort. They want to have access to the largest donors, both individuals and corporations, to gain support for library projects. Development professionals are beginning to see the value of library projects in attracting a wide variety of donors from diverse backgrounds as an opportunity to expand the total donor base for the campus.

Those involved in library development programs agree that academic library projects are exciting and have great impact on the quality of the overall educational experience at a college or university. Library projects, like few other campus programs, touch almost every individual student and faculty member and directly enhance the learning experience. This realization has prompted library directors and library development professionals to actively pursue fundraising efforts and seek the support of campus administrators.

CONVINCING RESULTS

Publications such as the *Chronicle of Higher Education*, library journals, and even *The New York Times*, tell many success stories of academic libraries getting measurable monetary results. At the 1991 spring DORAL meeting at Vanderbilt University, library development officers each reported their largest donation ever from an individual donor. The stories were impressive, ranging from an $800,000 gift to the University of California at Berkeley to a $20 million donation to the University of Florida. Eight other university libraries reported receiving gifts over $1 million.

Other examples of successful grants or corporate gifts include:

- $750,000 to the University of Iowa Libraries to build an interactive computer classroom/center from the Roy Carver Charitable Trust
- $240,000 to Northwestern University Library from the W.K. Kellogg Foundation to enhance library services to adult learners
- $6 million to Boise State University Library from Albertson's Inc. (supermarket chain) to renovate and expand its library.

Successes like these are encouraging academic libraries without development programs to start them. Once the decision to move ahead with a program is made, much groundwork needs to be accomplished with university officials.

POSITIONING THE LIBRARY

Enthusiasm for library development is not enough to ensure a successful program. The library must be seen as an integral part of the institutional mission, and it is up to the library director to make certain that this view of the library is accurate and apparent. How can this be accomplished? The library director, key librarians, and the library development staff (if the institution has a separate staff for this purpose) must all be involved in four key activities:

1. Educating
2. Networking
3. Strategic Planning
4. Implementing

EDUCATING THE UNIVERSITY ADMINISTRATION

No academic library development program will be successful without the support and understanding of key campus administrators. The library development program must be considered a high development priority for the entire campus in order to achieve real monetary results. Without this support, libraries will find it difficult to gain access to important individual and corporate donors and to be included in significant ways in institutional campaigns.

Obviously the support of the president of the college or university is absolutely critical. Educating the chief executive officer of the university about the library's programs and services is essential, but it can also be difficult. This busy and distracted administrator has little time to spend learning about the various constituencies on campus. Furthermore, the president, campus administrators, and faculty often consider themselves extremely knowledgeable about libraries. What more do they have to learn? The library director and staff must constantly find new opportunities to demonstrate the full range of the library's programs and services to this audience.

NETWORKING WITH KEY PEOPLE

Universities and colleges typically have a separate office devoted to development. The library director and library staff involved in development must become acquainted with the foundation or development office director. This individual is the key to sources of external funding, both individuals and corporations. The same is true of the campus grants office director, who coordinates grants from the federal government and sometimes large foundations such as Mellon and Ford.

STRATEGIC PLANNING

One way libraries are gaining support for more ambitious development efforts is through the campus strategic planning process. (For an example of a library strategic plan, see Appendix A on page xvi.) Libraries must learn to articulate their programs and associated budgetary needs clearly in terms of campus strategic priorities.

For example, the University of Iowa considers stronger undergraduate education a top strategic goal, and the University Libraries administration has responded by connecting some of its goals to this larger campus priority. They are expanding the library's user education programs, purchasing databases commonly used by undergraduates, and implementing new information technologies that support undergraduate courses.

IMPLEMENTATION

It is essential for those involved in library development efforts to obtain a comprehensive view of the field of fundraising and development. This can be accomplished in several ways:

- Visit or call an institution with a successful academic library development program and talk with key development personnel.
- Collect publications related to fundraising and grants from successful libraries or from the American Library Association library, which has a clearing house on fundraising materials.
- Attend workshops given by the American Library Association or the Council for the Advancement of Secondary Education.
- Read as much literature as possible on fundraising, especially library fundraising.

The library director should have a general understanding of major sources of funding—individuals, foundations, and corporations—for his or her part of the country. The director should take every opportunity to get to know state business leaders. A good working knowledge of federal government programs also is essential. The director should get to know key program officers of funding agencies and top officials of foundations and pay periodic visits to them armed with proposal ideas. This basic understanding will assist the director in making the case for funding both on and off the campus and in communicating more effectively with professional development staff.

The library director must provide leadership to help the library and/or development staff understand the development process. This can be achieved by:

- Providing staff development programs on the components, goals, and expected results of the library development effort.

- Encouraging attendance of key staff at library development continuing education programs.
- Identifying key library staff—assistant directors, special collections librarians, bibliographers, departmental librarians—and other staff who are good writers and/or speakers and involving them in the library development effort.

THE FUNDRAISING PROCESS

Each chapter of *Raising Money for Academic and Research Libraries* deals with a major component of the process, starting with the fundraising/development plan. Chapter 1 covers the critical importance of connecting overall institutional themes and goals with library fundraising efforts; elements of the planning process; the "case statement," the document which heightens awareness and tells the story of the library to the potential donor; prospect (potential donor) identification; and gift solicitation and acknowledgment.

Library friends groups are the focus of Chapter 2. The friends group is often the starting point for a comprehensive library development program, since it also serves as the key element in a library's annual giving program. Many of these donors also participate in a program of activities throughout the year. This group represents a loyal and productive constituency for the library.

An understanding of donor and donor relations, essential in the development of a successful library development program, is covered in Chapter 3. Knowing who potential donors are and why they give is a fundamental element in putting together a successful program. Academic libraries often have to justify their constituency bases because they do not have designated alumni in the same way that entire colleges or colleges within universities do. Other aspects covered in Chapter 3 include: categories of academic library donors; project selection based on the donor profile; solicitation methods for groups and individuals; and methods for donor recognition or stewardship.

Another important part of the academic library development program is the grants area, covered in Chapter 4. Federal and foundation grant opportunities exist for well defined and justified projects, particularly in areas such as preservation, materials acquisitions, automated bibliographic control, and capital projects. Knowing how to identify grant sources and how to construct proposals for specific audiences helps ensure a successful outcome. Specific information on federal and foundation grant sources for libraries is outlined, as well as detailed instruction for writing the grant proposal. Other issues covered include: gaining permission from the university to submit the grant; the grant review and reward process; the reporting process; and publicity strategies for successful grants.

Corporate giving has become a more important component of a successful library development program, supplementing individual, federal, and foundation sources. Chapter 5 discusses the natural connections between academic libraries and corporations; general trends in corporate philanthrology and the competition for corporate support; the importance of high level corporate volunteer leadership; opportunities for corporate giving; the factors by which many corporations rate projects.

The library campaign, a targeted fundraising effort for specific library projects, is probably the most focused and productive way to raise money for libraries and to harness the energies of such key people as campus administrators, foundation staff, library staff, faculty, students, and volunteers. Including the library in the college or university's campaign, however, can also be a major source of funds and donors in years to come. Planning and implementing a library campaign is a specialized skill that requires careful preparation. A detailed outline is given in Chapter 6. The "campaign with a campaign" is reviewed including how to present the library's case, how to identify and fulfilll personnel needs, and how to evaluate the campaign at its close.

Planned giving (or deferred giving) is becoming a larger and larger percentage of the total philanthropic dollar. This area, probably the most complicated and least understood in library development, is fully discussed in Chapter 7. More than just bequests, planned gift opportunities are now available for consideration by almost any age group and can immediately benefit the donor as well as the library. Library development professionals need to have some knowledge of the many planned gift opportunities that are mutually beneficial. Planned giving will become even more important as the U.S. population grows older. More kinds of deferred or planned gift programs are being developed each year to attract this rapidly growing segment of the population.

Successful library development efforts must be accompanied by a good public relations program. Chapter 8 explains how to develop and manage the public relations program: where to start, program plans, staffing, skills, and promotional ideas. The author discusses how a public relations program can be connected to the library's friends group; planning and creating effective publications—newsletters, brochures, and letters—that promote the library; and methods for effective use of the media.

Chapter 9 focuses on staffing and personnel issues for the library development program. Many libraries are now determining whether they need to devote a full- or part-time individual to these efforts. The author outlines duties and responsibilities of development officers in libraries, as well as professional associations, training programs, and organizations devoted to development in general and library development in particular.

The objectives of *Raising Money for Academic and Research Libraries* are to bring together the varied experience and expertise of 11 professionals in the field, to cover virtually every aspect of academic library development, and to offer all the essential practical information needed to proceed with a comprehensive development plan for the academic and research library.

APPENDIX A

UNIVERSITY OF IOWA LIBRARIES STRATEGIC PLAN OCTOBER 1, 1989

GOAL #8—DEVELOPMENT AND PUBLIC RELATIONS PROGRAMS INCREASE THE VISIBILITY OF UNIVERSITY LIBRARIES SERVICES AND COLLECTIONS TO NUMEROUS CONSTITUENCIES.

Objective A. Promote University Libraries collections and services to the community through a comprehensive public relations program and thereby increase general awareness of the value of the University Libraries to the State.

Strategy #1. Publicize events, collections, services, staff activities of the Libraries through diverse media approaches.

Strategy #2. Coordinate efforts with University Relations to effectively use the mass media on the local, state, regional and national level.

Strategy #3. Develop a coordinated and comprehensive publications series about the collections and services of the University Libraries.

Strategy #4. Continue to work with the Alumni Association to provide programs, as possible, for alumni groups visiting campus and at other locations.

Objective B. Increase the level of giving to the University Libraries by members of the University and by those outside the University community.

Strategy #1. Develop and sustain a program to establish a base for annual personal giving building on the Friends of the UI Libraries, and to encourage and generate corporate and foundation contributions.

Strategy #1a. Establish a new Development and Public Relations Advisory Committee.

Strategy #2. Continue to explore ways to make full use of IE 2000 campaign working closely with the University Foundation.

Strategy #3. Continue to work with Sponsored Programs and other departments to identify and secure federal funding as well as funding from private foundations and other sources.

Objective C. As a University intellectual and cultural center, the library initiates programs on diverse topics for a variety of audiences.

Strategy #1. Sustain and strengthen the exhibition/speaker series program.

Strategy #2. Initiate cooperative ventures with other University departments/programs to present symposia, lecture series, and related programs on timely topics.

1 FUNDRAISING/ DEVELOPMENT PLAN

by Mary Bailey Pierce

Fundraising as a professional process is best understood when viewed in its broader context—development. It begins with goal identification and ends with solicitation. Successful fundraisers are attuned to the "climate" for giving in their targeted donor groups and are well versed in the rules of planning, organizing and marketing to achieve a profitable outcome.

Libraries, large and small, will want to employ a diversified fundraising plan among private sources in order to meet their program goals. This means an annual fund program, a capital funds program and a deferred giving program. Annual funds are those monies received yearly from donors, usually for general support. Capital funds are those that support a specific project, or set of projects. Public funds at the national, state, and local levels are indeed available, though increasingly less so over the past decade. This chapter focuses on annual and capital programs. Public funding programs and deferred or planned giving are discussed in later chapters.

ELEMENTS OF THE PLAN

An effective fundraising plan for any library has three basic elements: a clear statement of the library's needs in the list of institutional goals; a library director with total commitment to fundraising priorities; and an approved expense budget adequate to meet fundraising objectives.

Most libraries will need a three-year plan that sets increasingly ambitious goals in terms of numbers of supporters and dollars. Implementing a three-year plan builds into each campaign the seeds of future success. Moreover, it develops a reliable corps of volunteers who can interpret the role and function of the library.

Volunteers are essential, particularly in the solicitation of the "big gift" and for personal contacts in the foundation and corporation world. Givers respond to conviction of purpose and to well-informed volunteers who are considered their peers. The staff provides the support and the planning framework for the volunteers. Even under the best of circumstances, however, there may be times when confusion over volunteer vs. staff roles will arise.

THE PLANNING PROCESS

BASIC STEPS

Defining organizational goals
Developing a plan
Statement of the case
Prospect identification, evaluation,
and motivation

DEFINING GOALS

The essential first step in fundraising, regardless of the size of the campaign, is to define the real needs of the library and what is required to meet those needs. During this phase the development officer, or staff member assigned to development, assembles facts from both internal and external sources or, if possible, uses the library's strategic plan to assess the future of the institution. In fact, fundraising is an excellent means for the library to meet certain of its defined program needs. Sometimes an outside consultant is hired to conduct a feasibility study at this point, especially for institution-wide fundraising efforts. The feasibility study, which consists in large part of a series of interviews with prospective donors, assesses the institution's potential for raising a designated level of funds.

Library staff, institutional trustees, officers, members of friends' groups, and as much of the general public as possible should be surveyed about the programmatic and financial goals to be met through any fundraising campaign. Your campaign will only succeed to the extent that staff, potential donors, and volunteer leaders support the purposes for which money is being sought.

THE INSTITUTIONAL SURVEY

The institutional survey helps define the library's current activities, explore what it should become, and identify programs that will move the institution toward its new objectives. Should the study identify any negative donor attitudes, the library will need to focus attention on a public relations campaign before undertaking any high-profile fundraising. While the survey is not meant to dictate overall programmatic goals to the library, it can reveal the most productive targets for fundraising efforts. Undoubtedly, there will be some overlap in all of the steps in this process. In the broad search for organizational goals, both prospective donors and volunteer leadership are likely to surface. Both can be sources of the key leadership gifts, which are so crucial to any successful campaign.

DEVELOPING A PLAN

The fundraising plan that evolves out of a careful organizational study should enjoy a higher than average success rate. Plans will vary in size and sophistication, depending upon the scope and content of the projected goals. The basis of the plan is the most important piece of literature that the campaign will produce—the case statement.

THE CASE STATEMENT

The case statement is the foundation on which all other campaign documents are based. The final version is often written by professional development staff in consultation with the library staff. Sometimes library staff write the initial drafts since they are closest to the issues. The statement is generally lengthy for it must be complete. It should tell a dynamic story of the history of the institution and its programs. It should heighten awareness of the possibilities for future benefits to the library, the university, and the community. Finally, it should "stir the reader to provide support for such an urgent and relevant cause."[1]

Whether the statement is prepared by a consultant, an individual, or a group of individuals, it is imperative to share the resulting draft with faculty, administrators, alumni, students, advisory boards, and others in the community in order to reach the broadest consensus possible. Regardless of the size or type of campaign, every case statement should describe what the library is, and the directions it should follow in the future.

The statement is an opportunity to enlighten those outside the library environment as well as library staff and friends on the history of the institution and its unique contributions. Libraries are historically saddled with many stereotypes. The case statement should explode those stereotypes, vigorously showcasing the abilities of staff and the record of program expansion. Moreover, it should clearly explain the efficiency of financial management that has sustained such growth with historically-limited resources— human and financial.

A financial statement forthrightly quantifying goals and documenting stewardship is particularly useful in uniting constituencies. When disparate prospective donors are led to agree on the combined goals and objectives of a campaign, it's future is virtually assured.

With the library's history, philosophy, and heritage well established, the case then turns to the real purpose of the statement—the future of the institution. Future needs are most appealing when they reaffirm current strengths to build toward a future that is relevant, important, and in keeping with new trends. The rationale for each new program must be presented to prospective donors in a manner that arouses pride of association, concern for continuity,

---

FIGURE 1-1 Case Statement Outline

I.   Preface

        Express the essence of your case in your opening statement
        and briefly highlight each goal. Sometimes this section is
        more easily written last--summarizing mission,
        accomplishment, future directions, and priority needs
        (Sections II through VI).

II.   Mission of the Library

        A.   Role in higher education and society

        B.   Collection goals and programs

        C.   Essential physical facilities

        D.   Philosophy of teaching and research

        E.   Factors of appeal to user needs:
                1.   Students and parents
                2.   Faculty and administrators
                3.   Trustees and volunteers
                4.   Friends and community
                5.   Past and potential donors

III.   Record of Accomplishment

        A.   Collection growth (i.e., volumes added, serials
                management, etc.)

        B.   Meeting user needs

        C.   Administrative structure:
                1.   Faculty and staff profile
                2.   Role in teaching/research

        D.   Improvement in physical facilities

FIGURE 1-1 *Continued*

    E.   Library services:
        1.   Public service
        2.   Technical processing

    F.   Distinctive gifts and supports

IV.   <u>Directions for Future</u>

    A.   Outstanding factors/programs that must continue

    B.   Users
        1.   How many people use the library?
        2.   User profile: who uses the collection?

    C.   Comprehensive collection development
        1.   Current serials
        2.   Archival collections

    D.   Library staffing

    E.   Physical facilities/new technologies

    F.   Budget needed for adequate support

V.   <u>Needs to Accomplish Directions/Objectives</u>

    A.   Possible priorities:
        1.   Physical facilities
        2.   Acquisitions
        3.   Interlibrary loan capability
        4.   Endowment

VI.   <u>Benefits to Community if Needs Are Met</u>

Note: This outline is furnished as a guide only, and all sections may not apply to your particular case. If followed, it should present a clear statement of your library, its current status, plans for the future, and how the audience for whom it is intended may contribute to its future.

and confidence. Seymour theorizes that the decision to give is first made emotionally and is then rationalized.[2]

Each project should have a target date and be ranked by priority as determined by the institution's master plan. Include a realistic financial estimate for each project, with a built-in inflation factor. The institution's long-range financial stability is at the heart of the master plan. That stability is assured only through endowment—some of the most difficult dollars to raise and surely among the most critical. Maintenance endowments for new buildings, for instance, are now regularly funded by foundations whose major focus is on capital improvements. Endowment of both faculty and program development are equally essential.

The packaging of the case statement will be determined by such important factors as the size of the campaign and the history and function of the institutions. For a blend of verbal and visual appeal, high quality design, layout, and writing are vital elements. A four-color statement rich in photographs may be very appropriate for a large academic library but a real turn-off for prospects of a smaller library.

Finally, the case statement is simply a means to an end, not the end itself. It is an evolving document that should be planned and written within the context of long-term program planning and development goals.

IDENTIFYING, EVALUATING AND MOTIVATING DONORS

Prospect or donor identification must start with the library's natural constituents (see Chapter 4). Not only are they the most likely to give, but few others will contribute to the cause until they do. Significant gifts rarely come from strangers. Most major donors are close friends of the institution or have logical reasons to support it. Research and evaluation is necessary to identify the most promising prospects, determine which ones will give and how much they might give, and which persons are the best ones to approach for gifts.[3]

This is precisely the process Benjamin Franklin used in 1749 when he set out to raise £5,000 to establish the academy that later became the University of Pennsylvania. He started by calling on his close friends and individuals with a strong desire to create such an institution. Those individuals provided Franklin's first—and largest—donations, and then helped him raise additional funds from their friends and colleagues. His efforts are the earliest recorded evidence of market segmentation in the fundraising process.

The prospect-research phase of fundraising is tedious and time consuming, causing many fundraisers to neglect or eliminate it. They do so at risk of failure. Research must be done with care and efficiency if a program is to succeed.

It is the function of development personnel to do the basic research, and then to involve selected leaders in an evaluation of probable levels of giving for peer-prospects. It is important to involve the people who will ultimately be leaders in the campaign and who will provide leadership gifts. They then develop an ownership attitude that helps make the campaign successful and broadens the base for future library appeals.

Each library will tailor its prospect research to its needs, the capabilities of its staff, and the kinds of prospects to be evaluated. In an annual campaign, for instance, staff will generally look to individuals and corporations simply because these two groups tend to favor gifts to annual programs while foundations are more interested in capital programs and long term projects.

In the capital campaign most gift income is derived from a small percentage of donors and research of prospects should be designed accordingly. A review of the history of capital campaigns, for instance, reveals that the top ten gifts consistently account for nearly one-third of the total raised; another third from the middle range of donors and the last third from all others. In the annual campaign, where gifts are much smaller, about 75 percent come from 25 percent of the donors. Each library should, therefore, look to its own special constituency for the nucleus of its prospects. That nucleus is subsequently canvassed for additional prospects. This process can produce a real sense of participation in the institutional community and is, moreover, a marvelous exercise in good public relations.

With a ratio of prospects to gifts of four to one, the importance of soliciting prospect names becomes self-evident. The evaluation process winnows the list down to the *real* prospects. Perhaps most important, a gift range table derived from this process will produce the most realistic goal for a campaign, whether annual or capital.

SETTING TIMETABLES

Precampaign procedures are paramount. It is what you do ahead of time and how it is done that usually decides whether you win or lose.[4] In the annual campaign, solicitations are limited to a period of four or five months. The campaign leadership or steering committee should be assembled and solicited at least six months prior to the public kickoff.

At the kickoff advance gifts are announced and sequential solicitation begun, followed by direct mail, telephone and special events fundraising. Four months later, when solicitations are completed, a victory dinner is held with appropriate recognition of campaign leadership. In the month following, the cycle begins again with selection of leadership for the next year's campaign.

The timetable for the capital campaign is generally three to five years. In the first year of critical precampaign procedures *the* most significant is that of engaging an independent consultant to conduct a feasibility study. This helps determine the potential for the capital funding program approved by the chief executive officer and the trustees.

BUILDING THE TEAM

Upon recommendation to proceed, a campaign goal is set and a steering committee and campaign chairperson are appointed. They and the trustees are solicited and they, in turn, identify a prospect for a major challenge gift of at least 25 percent of total goal. Chapter 3 gives some helpful hints on how to recruit the most effective individuals for this purpose.

After one year, with at least 25 percent of pledges secured, the campaign is publicly announced. Personal solicitation for major gifts begins, immediately followed by special-gift solicitations. Two years of general gift and mail solicitation complete the sequential campaign. The latter two may be expected to produce limited return to a capital effort, but cultivate important support for subsequent annual campaigns.

REPORTING, ACKNOWLEDGING, AND STEWARDSHIP

Adequate support systems are indispensable tools in fundraising. Recording systems contribute significantly to a successful program. Four basic functions are required:

- Donor records
- Periodic gift reports
- Gift acknowledgment
- Data processing

Prospect information should be held in a secure location and always treated as confidential. It can give staff the best information available for evaluating prospect gift levels. An effective donor records system is the source of all pledge-billing information, maximizing campaign solicitation efforts. It also helps prevent the embarrassment of duplicate solicitation. Periodic gift reports are much-needed benchmarks of the program's progress.

Gifts should be acknowledged promptly. For smaller gifts a receipt is usually adequate. Gifts above a set amount require a personal acknowledgment from the chief executive officer that includes assurances of appropriate designation or restriction.

Data processing in today's library is synonymous with computer programming. Smaller libraries can benefit from shared systems, which minimize computer costs. The volume of storage and speedy retrieval are valuable tools in decision-making throughout the campaign. Organizational needs will dictate the kind of system—manual or electric—that assures fundraising success.

THE BIG PICTURE

According to the American Association for Fund Raising Counsel (AAFRC), giving to education rose to $10.69 billion in 1989, an increase of 4.5 percent over the $10.23 billion donated in 1988. Of that amount an estimated $8.925 billion went to higher education. After adjusting for inflation, however, gifts to education showed no growth from 1988 to 1989.[5]

The philanthropic sector is shifting attention to the nation's elementary and secondary schools. This changing focus is driven by the widespread perception that these schools are insufficiently preparing students for competitive participation in a shrinking global economy.

The F.W. Olin Foundation (whose major program focus is capital improvement) has reported that it would cost $60 billion to rectify the "decaying infrastructure" of U.S. colleges and universities. The report warned that the inadequacy of libraries and computer equipment, as well as deteriorating buildings, threatens the future quality of higher education.[6]

Competition for the philanthropic dollar is intense. Other persons of conviction and ability are also seeking donors whose goals match those of their organizations. With the economy in difficulty, with community needs growing at a rapid pace, and with more sophisticated development techniques, library fundraising must be skillfully and professionally planned to meet the needs of the organization.

ENDNOTES

1. Harold J. Seymour, *Designs for Fund-Raising*, New York: McGraw Hill, 1966. p. 22.
2. Ibid. p. 29.
3. Thomas E. Broce, *Fund Raising*, University of Oklahoma Press, 1979. p. 153.
4. Seymour, p. 37
5. American Association of Fund Raising Counsel, *Giving, USA: 1990 Annual Report*, New York: AAFRC, 1990.
6. "Decaying American Campus: A Ticking Time Bomb," *FRM Weekly*, April 26, 1989.

2 LIBRARY FRIENDS

by Joan M. Hood

A library is the heart of an educational institution, whether public or private, large or small. Library friends organizations have existed for decades to assist libraries by providing additional sources of revenue, by increasing visibility, and by working as advocates.

Personal and private support for academic libraries existed long before the formal establishment of library friends organizations. From their beginnings in the United States, academic libraries have enjoyed the support of innumerable friends. The oldest example is Harvard University, named for John Harvard in recognition of his bequest of 400 books and half of his estate in 1638.

Yale University's librarian, James T. Babb, often told the story of the founding of Yale College. According to tradition, ten Congregational ministers met in the home of the Reverend Samuel Russel in 1701. Each clergyman brought choice volumes from his personal library. As the ministers gathered around a table in Mr. Russel's home, each one placed his particular contribution on the table and intoned the words "I give these books for the founding of a college in this colony."[1]

Edward G. Holley, Dean Emeritus of the School of Library Science at the University of North Carolina at Chapel Hill and distinguished library historian, suggests that it is no accident that Harvard and Yale today have the two largest university libraries in this country. "From the beginning there was a recognition of the principal that books and libraries are indispensable for the advancement of scholarship, culture, and learning." Dean Holley adds that "no library has ever achieved significance without the support of those who understand that principal, whether they be librarians, faculty, donors, administrators, or legislators. Libraries exist because of those who understand their mission, who are sympathetic to that mission, and who find it their moral, political, and economic support."[2]

The first university library friends organization was founded at Harvard in 1925. It most likely was modeled on the first library support organization to call itself a friends group, La Societe des Amis de la Bibliotheque Nationale et des Grandes Bibliotheques de France which had been founded in 1913, and with which Harvard's library director, Archibald Coolidge, had become familiar during a book-buying expedition to Europe.[3] By 1930 there were other library friends groups at eastern private colleges.

In analyzing the growth of friends groups from the 1930s to the present, it is obvious that there are fluctuations in the number of organizations. The number grows during periods of financial constraint and shrinks when there is ample funding. The golden age for higher education in this country was the 1950s and part of the 1960s. We began to see a downturn in funding in the 1970s that accelerated in the 1980s. True to form we have seen an explosion of development activities in academic libraries in the last ten years, and in public universities during the last five years. Trend spotters predict that the number one priority of higher educational institutions in the 1990s will be adequate funding. Libraries will be in the midst of this quest for additional revenue sources.

Historically at academic libraries, friends groups were formed to support special collections, rare books or a narrowly defined interest such as fine printing. While this support and interest remains a valid and vital one at most universities, it has become essential for many friends groups to broaden the base of their support, especially if one of their major purposes is fundraising. As mentioned earlier, library friends can play multiple roles in assisting an academic library. A friends organization can assist in: increasing visibility through publications and programs; identifying and soliciting individuals, corporations and foundations for financial contributions and gifts-in-kind; and lobbying for an increase in the tax base for a public institution.

ORGANIZATION

The library friends organization at an academic institution can be a separate not-for-profit or 501(C)(3) organization, or it can be part of a university foundation, if one exists at a particular university. The friends' board of directors establishes policy for the organization. It must be very clear that the group does not establish policy for the library.

There are many acceptable types of organizations that can be tailored to the needs of a particular college or university. Despite the structure, it is important to achieve a good balance of community, faculty, and alumni representation. It is always a good idea to include an attorney on the board. The bylaws should specify rotation of board members to foster the development of new ideas for the organization.

A committee structure should be established first, although the actual committees may vary according to the activities of the organization. Examples of committees in friends organizations are:

Development
Membership
Program
Volunteer services

Many friends organizations have a five-year planning committee to develop, with the library faculty and staff, a written plan containing goals and objectives. This provides the necessary framework to formulate, administer, and later analyze agreed upon plans.

At the University of Illinois Library at Urbana-Champaign, the library friends organization works closely with the University Office of Development and Public Affairs. The development officer for annual funds is the staff liaison with the library friends board of directors. Figure 2-1 illustrates the organizational structure. Providing staff support for the library friends organization is an important activity of the Development Office.

UNIVERSITY OF ILLINOIS FRIENDS

In 1972 at Illinois the library administration recognized the need to expand private support and public visibility. Although the State of Illinois had provided adequate support through much of the library's history, the 1970s brought budgetary constraints and record inflation. It became difficult to keep the collection current, much less purchase the special items needed for research and instruction.

The University of Illinois Library Friends at Urbana-Champaign was established in 1972 to attract annual private funds for the library's acquisitions and services and to establish dialogue with users, donors, and volunteers. In the first year Library Friends numbered 312 charter members who donated $7,800. For the next several years the number of members remained constant, in the range of 300 donors who generated between $10,000 to $13,000 annually. It was only when the library administration made the decision to employ a Library Friends Coordinator whose sole responsibility was the development of the annual funds program that significant growth occurred. In 1977/1978 membership increased by a third and income doubled to $20,000. Since 1977 steady growth has occurred. In fiscal year 1990, nearly 4,000 donors generated more than $330,000 in annual funds. When major gifts are added, private support for the Library totaled more than $2.3 million in FY90. Library Friends donors are drawn from every state in the United States and from more than ten foreign countries.

The Coordinator's position is now full-time and is titled Development Officer for Annual Funds. For a large friends organization a full-time position is ideal, although many organizations cannot start with a full-time person. At Illinois the position grew from 50 percent of full-time from 1977 to 1980, to 65 percent in 1980, and to 100 percent in 1986.

Because of the success of the annual funds program (known as Library Friends), the library in 1981 established an Office of Development and Public Affairs staffed by a full-time director. The goals of the office are to promote private financial growth through the addition of a major donor program and to develop a network of support nationwide. Library Friends, the annual funds program, plays a vital role in the library's total long-range development program. The public affairs component complements the development responsibility, because greater visibility increases public awareness of the library and concomitantly increases private support.

Illinois successfully moved a narrowly-defined local support group interested solely in special collections into a national organization that supports the entire library system. This broad support is vital for the long-term growth of the organization.

Categories of membership vary reflecting the individual nature of the group. Generally they incorporate some of the following levels:

$1,000	Benefactor
500	Patron
100	Sponsor
60	Subscribing Member
30	Contributing Member
15	Student Member

Levels of support greater than the $1,000 contribution are often recognized in specially named groups that incorporate the history and tradition of the institution.

Gift of Membership: Many friends enjoy making a gift of membership to their friends and colleagues. This opportunity can be especially appropriate for birthdays, anniversaries, and holidays.

Memorial Gifts: A special program of many library friends organizations is the memorial fund. It provides tangible recognition of gifts in memory of family, friends, and colleagues. Many friends organizations design special bookplates that are inserted in newly-purchased items. An announcement of the gift is sent from the friends office to the family.

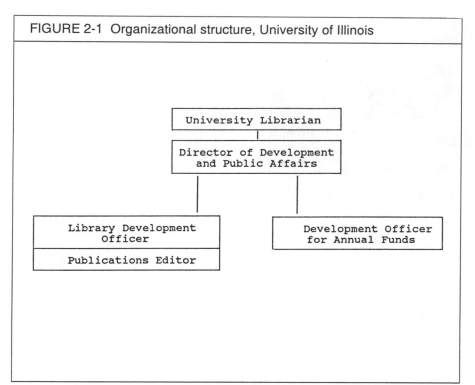

Memorial Gift Books and Books as Tributes

University of Illinois Library Friends at Urbana-Champaign

Tributes: Friends often make gifts as tributes to others to commemorate important events such as birthdays, anniversaries, graduations, and retirements. A distinctive bookplate is usually inserted in the acquired material.

FIGURE 2-1 Organizational structure, University of Illinois

University Librarian

Director of Development and Public Affairs

Library Development Officer

Publications Editor

Development Officer for Annual Funds

MEMBERSHIP AND BENEFITS

In addition to a personal contribution to the library's excellence, library friends throughout the country help stimulate the creation of programs of activities. During each academic year lectures and exhibits related to acquired collections are sponsored by library friends. Members are invited to previews of new acquisitions and to receptions honoring special guests of the library. Friends in the immediate area also have an opportunity to help as volunteers. Friends groups might include other benefits such as:

- Special circulation privileges for library materials
- Newsletters
- Annual reports
- Friends-only preview of the library's annual book sale
- Discounts on university publications

FRIENDS OF THE SMU LIBRARIES
C O L O P H O N
FINE BOOK AUCTION

Monday, April 24, 1989
6:00 P.M.
DeGolyer Estate
Dallas Arboretum

PROGRAMS

Each semester library friends organizations sponsor major programs for their members. Many universities attract noted authors and speakers to present talks. Cleveland State University in Ohio organized a scholars and artists reception. The event recognized the scholarly and creative accomplishments of the faculty and staff of the university through a public exhibit of their works.

The University of California at San Diego Library Friends established a Great Authors Series. They invite well known authors to give public lectures on campus. Ancillary development activities are built into the schedule of events.

In Dallas, the Friends of Southern Methodist University held a Fine Book Auction which attracted a large number of participants. The Northwestern University Library Council sponsors annual book fairs.

The University of Illinois Library Friends sponsored a benefit to raise funds to restore its original Audubon Elephant Folio. This successful project raised more than $93,000.

At Texas A&M University, the Sterling C. Evans Library Friends held a Boots and Books party to celebrate Texas authors and country/western music.

*Library Friends
Annual Report*
University of Illinois Library at Urbana-Champaign

The Ohio State University Friends sponsored a birthday party to honor Walt Kelly, creator of the *Pogo* cartoon strip.

Library programming also offers an excellent opportunity to cooperate with many university units. Because the library encompasses all academic disciplines and units of a university, the possibilities for cooperative ventures are endless.

COMMUNICATION

A good communications program is necessary to a successful development and public affairs effort. Most library friends organizations sponsor a variety of publications. A regular newsletter is a vital piece of communication. The newsletter should be sent to donors, prospective donors, and selected audiences. The issues can feature major library events, notable acquisitions, information about donors, and a variety of regular columns.

An annual publication can highlight the library's collections, services, and personnel in more depth than is possible in a newsletter. A financial statement of the friends organization should be presented in addition to pertinent library financial information.

An important segment of the annual report is a list by giving category of all donors to library friends during the fiscal year. Donors need to be recognized, especially at the upper giving levels. Alphabetical listings of donors do not have the impact of listings by giving categories. If you list the names of donors, make sure your lists are accurate. Mistakes can be costly to development and public affairs efforts.

EXHIBITION CATALOGS

Many friends groups support the publication of exhibition catalogs that are published in conjunction with exhibits to which friends are invited. Individual major donors to publications can be recognized within the publication as well as general funds such as those donated in a pool by library friends. Since 1986 the Association of College and Research Libraries division of the American Library Association has been sponsoring an annual exhibition catalog competition. In 1990 the Thomas Fisher Rare Book Library of the University of Toronto was cited for its series of 23 distinguished catalogs, issued free of charge over a five-year period, which show a consistently impressive scholarly achievement with permanent reference value.

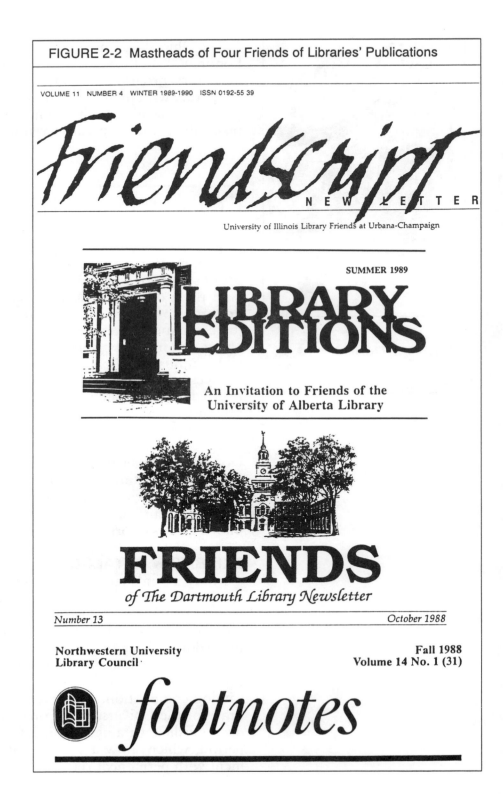

FIGURE 2-2 Mastheads of Four Friends of Libraries' Publications

AUDIOVISUAL PRESENTATIONS

Video technology has given library friends new opportunities to tell about the library. Videocassettes can be used on a one-to-one basis with individual donors, with small groups or with a large screen for large group presentations. A public affairs component can be woven in with a development component if resources do not allow the production of two separate tapes. Such tapes can also be used for faculty and staff presentations, especially for new personnel orientations.

TOURS

Many libraries conduct tours for new faculty and students at the beginning of each semester and for individual guests to the library. A friends project can be the production of a tour on a portable cassette player. At Illinois one side of the tape features the undergraduate library, the second side the main library. Each tour is accompanied by a map of the section featured. The tour cassettes may be checked out at the media center in the undergraduate library and the information desk in the circulation area of the main library.

VOLUNTEERS

Volunteers are effective spokespeople for the library because they have no vested interest. Volunteers are a vital part of every nonprofit organization, and libraries are no exception. Cynthia Wedel, Vice President of the World Council of Churches, has had a distinguished career working with volunteers. She feels that there are three categories of volunteers, all of whom can be useful:

- Policy-making volunteers—the ones who serve on boards and committees—are generally well organized and busy. They should be chosen carefully and allowed to play an active role in policy making.
- Management volunteers make good committee chairpersons with specific assignments to supervise.
- Service volunteers—the ones who do the hands-on work— may make significant contributions without taking on long-term project or management tasks.

Because volunteers require an investment of time and energy, the library must be sure that it is committed to a volunteer program. Most volunteers serve part-time. Job descriptions for the tasks that need to be accomplished are an important management tool.

Planned recognition of volunteers is also essential. Each year a

Gifts from Our Friends

An Exhibition to Celebrate the
Fifth Anniversary of the
Friends of the
Thomas Fisher Rare Book Library

January 1990

recognition program should be scheduled to honor the library's service volunteers. All volunteers should receive a certificate or similar memento as a tangible recognition of their service. Volunteer activities can be highlighted in friends newsletters.

Like other segments of a public relations and development program, a volunteer effort must be sustained over a period of time. As volunteers become more involved in the work of the library, they become invaluable to expansion of services and programs. The friends' volunteer service program can include special projects which neither the library staff nor students are able to maintain on a regular basis. For example, "reading the shelves" to ensure the proper location of materials, locating materials which have increased in value and should be reassigned to more secure areas, cleaning and oiling the leather bindings of volumes in the rare book and special collections library, or leading tours of visiting groups. Specific projects in departmental libraries can draw on the diverse interests of volunteers. The library friends board of directors that makes policy for the annual funds program is a vital volunteer function.

FUNDRAISING

The key words in fundraising are identification, cultivation, and solicitation—all the results of careful planning, patience, and continuity. One does not begin any kind of development operation expecting instant results. Professional staff directing the efforts of a volunteer group can develop an annual funds program that will build a financial base over time.

In organized fundraising, a good way to begin is to learn as much as one can about people. Harold Seymour, who wrote the classic text *Design for Fund Raising*, pointed out two universal human aspirations:

> "What people want most is to be sought, to be asked to participate."

> "Every individual needs to feel that he or she is a worthwhile member of a worthwhile group."[4]

Pride of association and the responsible concern for continuity are two additional basic motivators for people. He points out that

Bookplate for the E. Kenneth Gray Endowment Fund, reflecting Dr. Gray's love of fishing.

a donor's main motivation to give is the opportunity to reinforce his or her self image as a person helping to solve a problem in society.

Libraries are the source of information for people solving society's problems. They also provide continuity in our society. Therefore, I believe that the fundraising potential for libraries is enormous, because they provide the basic ingredients for people helping to solve problems in society.

IDENTIFICATION

The identification of donors for libraries, especially for academic libraries, presents a unique problem. No one has graduated from the library system. On the other hand, one hopes that all alumni availed themselves of the resources provided by the library. Libraries must strongly defend the right of access to all alumni of the institution. It is essential that this policy be determined at the highest campus level. Otherwise, the library will find that it has no development market. As fundraising efforts develop in colleges and other units at a university, libraries often find they become involved in "turf wars." A particular college may wish to limit access to its own graduates. It is imperative that a library have access to the entire alumni body for fundraising.

CULTIVATION

Cultivation of donors and prospective donors can be achieved successfully through programs that were discussed earlier, such as exhibition openings, previews of new acquisitions, and receptions honoring special guests. In order to attract potential donors it is a good idea to invite the public at large. Many institutions have found that it is more helpful for the friends to be an inclusive group rather than an exclusive organization.

Special events such as dedicating new physical properties or highlighting a special acquisition such as a millionth volume, present unlimited possibilities. It is always a good idea to include high ranking university administrators to participate in special activities. By involving the friends board, the library is providing a valuable vehicle of communication for the university with the lay community.

SOLICITATION

An annual funds program is the core of the development effort. Recruiting and training volunteers, upgrading donors, and building a broad base of ongoing support are critical to the overall development program. Three traditional methods of solicitation are:

1. Direct mail
2. Telefunds or phonathons
3. Personal meetings

They are listed in ascending order of effectiveness. It is easiest, but least effective, to solicit by mail. Phonathons tend to be more costly, but they provide a higher percentage of response and a larger dollar return. Personal solicitations are the most effective method. Meeting with an individual has immediate feedback and usually results in larger gifts. All nonprofit organizations and certainly all libraries adapt these methods to their own organizations.

Determining the best system of solicitation for a specific project is the Library's most important step. The objective is always the same—obtaining the highest dollar return for the smallest dollar expenditure.

DIRECT MAIL

Many books and articles have been written about direct mail. It is important to read about the varying factors that determine the success of a direct mail appeal; however, regardless of how careful the plans, a 1- to 3-percent response rate is the best you can expect for new donor acquisition. Direct mail for gift renewal should generate a high percentage return. New donor acquisition is always the most costly part of an annual funds program. Therefore, great care should be taken to retain those donors once you have them. Good record keeping is vital. Library friends donors may be renewed on the anniversary date of their earlier gift, or they may be renewed at a specific time in the calendar year. Most academic friends groups now rely on computerized data systems to renew contributions on a timely basis.

TELEFUNDS

Telefunds or phonathons are a much more successful means of acquiring new donors. A 20- to 25-percent pledge rate from prospective donors is not unusual, however, it is much more costly to conduct a telefund than a direct mail campaign. Because of the substantial initial investment, it is even more important to make sure that the net proceeds are worth the expense and that every effort is made to retain the new donors in future years.

Telefunds can be especially effective during a special project such as a challenge grant. Degree-granting units of a university often run a telefund with their students working either as volunteers or as paid callers. Because the library does not have a body of students on which to draw, some academic library friends organizations have successfully contracted with their respective university foundation or with a private vendor.

PERSONAL SOLICITATION

Volunteers or staff members who call on prospects in person to solicit major contributions will need to be recruited and trained carefully. A volunteer who solicits major gifts should be a major donor him or herself and should have given an amount equal to that for which the prospect is being asked. Networks of volunteers can be established with each volunteer being assigned a specific number of solicitations. Some members of friends boards find this activity an especially appropriate way for them to serve the library. Others prefer to provide different kinds of services. It is important for the staff to know which members can be successful fundraisers.

SPECIAL PROJECTS

Academic libraries are often the recipients of grants from agencies such as the National Endowment for the Humanities (NEH), a state humanities organization, or from private corporations or foundations. Members of friends boards and organizations can help immeasurably to identify and to solicit donors for these projects if a matching component is part of the grant. A major grant such as an NEH Challenge Grant is a special opportunity. The friends organizations at Johns Hopkins University, the University of California at San Diego, and the University of Illinois at Urbana-Champaign are actively involved in helping their respective libraries meet current challenge grant requirements. The friends group at Brown University helped that institution successfully complete a challenge grant.

ENDOWED BOOK FUNDS

Endowed book funds recognizing a specific donor are a natural extension of an annual funds program. Every university has basic requirements regarding the establishment of a named endowment fund. For many libraries the minimum amount is $10,000. By publicizing this giving opportunity, libraries have been able to establish an ongoing source of support for different sections of their collections. Usually a special bookplate is designed and inserted in all material purchased with the income from the endowed fund. The Stanford University Library has a special publication to keep donors and the families of donors informed

Library
of the
University of Illinois
at Urbana-Champaign

Acquired through
The Evelyn E. Pflaum Endowment
In Memory of Her Daughter
Barbara Lynn Pflaum

Each endowed book fund has a bookplate specially designed for it, often reflecting the interests of the honoree.

and involved with the selection of material to be purchased with a specific fund.

GIFTS-IN-KIND
Gifts-in-kind are a constant source of support for libraries. Many of these materials can be added to the collection. Library friends groups often organize book sales to raise money from the duplicates and titles not appropriate for a particular collection.

PLANNED GIVING
Planned giving offers libraries the best source of continuing income over a long time period. While most donors have limits on the amount of money that they can give during their lifetimes, planned giving offers excellent opportunities for donors to make significant contributions. Gifts can be made to a library through bequests as well as through planned giving vehicles such as charitable remainder unitrusts, annuities, and pooled income funds.

SUMMARY

In all of these efforts library friends are invaluable. They can publicize the strengths of the library far more credibly than anyone who works for the library, because they have no vested interest in its operation, and because they often have a wider circle of acquaintances and influence. They are the core of the development program.

Development is a process carried out over years and decades and must not be regarded as a short-term project. Sometimes the annual contributions of a friends group scarcely justify its existence in the beginning, but over a period of time the annual fund grows to support not only its own program, but to become the critical factor in the longer term investment of bequests, significant donations of gifts-in-kind, capital programs, and the building of endowment funds. By carefully cultivating a variety of sources, libraries have gained better collections, better support, and better service for their patrons throughout the country.

ENDNOTES

1. James T. Babb, "The Yale University Library," *Library Trends* 15, Oct. 1966: 206.
2. Edward G. Holley, "The Library and Its Friends," *Organizing the Library's Support: Donors, Volunteers, Friends*, University of Illinois Graduate School of Library Science, 1980: 10.
3. Sarah L. Wallace, ed., *Friends of the Library: Organization and Activities*, Chicago, ALA, 1962: 4.
4. Harold J. Seymour, *Designs for Fund-Raising*, McGraw-Hill, New York, 1966.

RECOMMENDED READING

Breivik, Patricia Senn and E. Burr Gibson, eds. *Funding Alternatives for Libraries*. American Library Association, Chicago, 1979.

Dolnick, Sandy, ed. *Friends of Libraries Sourcebook*. American Library Association, Chicago, 1980.

Dolnick, Sandy, ed. *Fundraising for Nonprofit Institutions. Foundations in Library and Information Science*. Volume 19, JAI Press Inc., Greenwich, CT, 1987.

Dove, Kent E. *Conducting a Successful Capital Campaign*. Jossey-Bass Publishers, San Francisco, CA, 1988.

Krummel, D. W., ed. *Organizing the Library's Support: Donors, Volunteers, Friends*, University of Illinois Graduate School of Library Science, Urbana-Champaign, IL, 1980.

Pray, Francis C. *Handbook for Educational Fundraising*. Jossey-Bass, Inc., San Francisco, 1981.

The Public Management Institute. *Managing Volunteers for Results*. San Francisco, CA, 1977.

———. *Successful Fund Raising Techniques*. San Francisco, CA, 1977.

Seymour, Harold J. *Designs for Fund-Raising*. McGraw-Hill Inc., New York, 1966.

Smith, Virginia Carter, ed. *Currents*. Council for the Advancement and Support of Education, Washington, D.C.

Wilson, Marlene. *The Effective Management of Volunteer Programs*. Johnson Publishing Company, Boulder, CO, 1981.

3 DONOR AND DONOR RELATIONS

by Charlene Clark

Donors and donor relations are subjects covered extensively in fundraising and development journals, but rarely discussed in library journals. This lack of information leaves the impression that libraries and library journals put more emphasis on the gift and the getting of the gift than they do on the giver of the gift. However, the more likely reason for this lapse is not a lack of concern, but a lack of knowledge. As relative newcomers to fundraising, librarians have simply not had enough collective experience to develop donor relations programs on a large scale, let alone to write about them. Articles on library fundraising tend to focus on events and strategies rather than on the people who make the gifts, leading one to believe that donors are a scarce, elusive lot and that very little is known about them. In fact, quite the opposite is true.

There are no gifts to libraries or any other organizations without donors. They make it all happen. To emphasize the gift over the giver is a grave mistake as all seasoned fundraisers know. In the introduction to his classic study, *Designs for Fund Raising,* Harold J. Seymour, dean of fundraising observes, "The story of fund raising begins and ends with people. . . . Every cause . . . needs people more than money."[1] The key to successful fundraising is donor literacy. The golden rule of fundraising is, quite simply, "Know your donors." Just as libraries were in the vanguard of computer literacy, they must now take up the mission of donor literacy if they are to succeed in fundraising.

DONOR PROFILE

Donors to libraries have much in common with other donors, and are likely to be donors to other organizations or institutions as well. Although donors may vary greatly in personality and interests, they tend to fit a known profile. Despite the all too familiar warning about the dangers of generalizing, some valid generalizations about the common characteristics of donors and their motives for giving can be made. Veteran fundraiser Kent Dove, author of *Conducting a Successful Capital Campaign: A Comprehensive Fund Raising Guide for Non Profit Organizations,* enumerates the following traits of major donors:

1. They are religious.
2. They are conservative.
3. They believe in free enterprise.
4. They have strong beliefs and values.
5. They know something about the organizations to which they give.
6. They are very opinionated.
7. They believe in what the organization stands for and they have values similar to the organization or institution.
8. They view giving as an investment in the future of an institution.
9. They accept but do not seek recognition.
10. They remain faithful to their favorite charities.[2]

While scholarly information on donors may not appear in professional journals, library newsletters are filled with articles on donors and their gifts. Lists of donors appear regularly in most newsletters and annual reports of academic libraries. Stories praising major gifts with pictures of smiling donors are an important part of library newsletters and promotional publications, even if they are not part of the professional literature. With increased promotional activities and publications stressing library needs and publicizing gifts, the ranks of library donors are swelling. Effective public relations not only attracts donors but retains them and is a central part of any donor relations program.

Although library donors do share common traits with other kinds of donors, their appreciation of the library and its crucial role in supporting academic programs is what sets them apart. Traditionally library donors have been lovers of books and the printed word. They have given primarily to support collections. However, in a world increasingly dependent on technology, a growing number are becoming avid supporters of information and information access.

Donors to academic libraries are part of a larger group of institutional donors and are often already supporting other academic units within the university, such as liberal arts or engineering. Their other giving interests should be considered when developing proposals. Projects that satisfy their interests in subject or curriculum areas such as humanities or engineering will often be the most appealing projects. They allow the donors to remain loyal to their colleges while strengthening the library's holdings in that area.

The greatest impediment to fundraising in academic libraries is the lack of a natural constituency within the institution. Donors to an institution are most likely alumni whose natural inclination is to support the college from which they took their degree. Since the library is used by all but grants degrees to none, it is likely to be "out of sight and out of mind" to most institutional donors. The academic library has long suffered from an identity crisis within the institutional environment. Alumni and prospective donors have to be told emphatically and repeatedly that the library is central to the university's teaching and research missions and that it needs private support. After the message is articulated regularly at the highest levels, donors respond eagerly with gifts. With effective promotion, the identity crisis can be overcome and a constituency developed. The challenge to the library in the long term is to strengthen ties with students who are dependent on the library now and who will be the donors of the future. Strategies for accomplishing this through projects such as class gifts will be discussed later.

ALL DONORS GREAT AND SMALL

Unlike the academic colleges that concentrate on a few large gifts primarily for scholarships, fellowships, and endowed chairs, libraries need both large and small gifts: from $500 to $5,000,000. Every donor is important to the library regardless of the size of the gift. There may be small donors, but there are no minor donors. While development efforts concentrate on the wealthier donors, small givers should not be ignored. Fundraisers agree that past donors are the best prospects for future gifts. The pool of major donors is likely to grow from those who are already making smaller gifts. Loyalty is an intrinsic motive for giving. A Friends member who contributed $100 a year for the last five years or $500 in one year could become a prospect for a major gift. Time and effective donor research will tell.

A growing pool of major donors is the ultimate aim of all library development programs. Defining the level of a major gift varies greatly from library to library and is entirely dependent on the library's capacity for getting gifts. Some libraries may define a major donor as one who gives at least $1000. Others may define a major donor as someone who gives at least $5000 or even $10,000. A $100,000 gift is a common occurrence at some libraries, while it may be a once in a lifetime event at others. The amount of the gift is not so important as is the treatment of the donor. A donor who is appreciated will give again. A library's skill at fundraising is measured by its ability to get the next gift. Only donors who are well treated and appreciated will give again. Every library should determine what it considers a major donor level and establish meaningful ways of recognizing donors who make gifts at above that level.

DONOR CATEGORIES

Regardless of the size of their gifts, donors to academic libraries can be sorted into broad categories. Segmenting donors by categories is important because it tells us who the donors are, where they are to be found, and how to approach them. The following is a list of general categories from which donors are likely to come:

1. Alumni, their spouses and family
2. Parents of current students
3. Board members
4. External support organizations (such as alumni clubs and parents clubs)
5. Graduating and reunion classes
6. Collectors
7. Faculty
8. Friends members
9. Former student workers in the library
10. Student groups (such as fraternities and sororities)
11. Maverick donors

ALUMNI

Clearly, some donors will fall into several categories. Most prospective and current donors, however, will be alumni who have actively supported the institution at least through membership in the alumni association. Many are already volunteer leaders serving on alumni boards or as officers in local alumni organizations. Their positions within the alumni hierarchy are important, for they can articulate the library's message, arrange for presentations about the library to large groups, and generally influence others to make gifts.

SPOUSES

Spouses figure prominently in decisions about major gifts and should always be considered when building a relationship with a prospective donor. Spouses and family members of alumni are likely prospects for gifts, particularly if the alumni member has previously supported the library. In the case of a deceased alumnus, the spouse or family members may feel a strong obligation to carry on the tradition of giving to the library and may be prospects for a major gift, particularly a memorial. If the deceased alumnus's interest in the library was keen and other key factors are favorable, surviving family members may wish to bestow a planned gift or bequest.

WOMEN

Considering spouses raises the pertinent issue of donor gender. Women (alumnae and others) are gaining in prominence as donors, and institutions are taking note of that fact.[3] Women have long been effective in the role of volunteers and have in fact been the backbone of many library volunteer efforts, especially the friends. Libraries should be alert to the potential for increased giving from women and to their influence on major gift decisions. Women not only influence their spouses in making major gifts, they also influence their companies and other groups with which they are affiliated. Charles Haight, associate vice president for development at Yale University observes, "Women have been very active as class agents, helping to raise money."[4] No longer backstage volunteers, women are assuming an advocacy role which puts them in the forefront of fundraising. Corporate women are effective advocates in lobbying for corporate gifts. Libraries should look at groups dominated by women and seek ways to win their support. In the matter of women as donors, fund raiser Jerold Panas, author of *Mega Gifts,* offers this advice: "In every regard, in raising funds, I would approach women precisely the same way I would approach men."[5]

PARENTS

Parents, like alumni, are obvious prospects for library gifts. Their giving to the university is likely to reflect the interests of their children and is typically directed toward student activities and programs. Since the library is a key part of their child's educational career, they are very responsive to library appeals, but primarily at the lower levels of giving. They may be excellent prospects for long term cultivation, but their capacity to give is often limited by the expenses of putting their children through college. The library has the opportunity, however, to build a relationship based on smaller gifts, such as through the friends, that may produce a major gift in later years.

BOARD MEMBERS

Individuals who serve on external development or advisory boards for the library are excellent prospects for library gifts since they are informed about the library's needs and aspirations. The golden rule for board members is "give, get, or get off." In fundraising it is mandatory for board members to be able to give or get a gift. If they are unable or unwilling to do either of these things, they should resign. Board members are chosen for leadership and their ability to influence others. One of the obligations of leadership is financial support for the cause. Panas believes so firmly "the buck starts with the board," that he selects the phrase as his title for the chapter on board memberships in *Mega Gifts*.[6]

GROUPS AND ORGANIZATIONS

In the quest for donors, libraries should consider groups and organizations as well as individuals. Individuals with an interest in the library are likely to belong to organizations that are also potential donors. Alumni groups and parents clubs are prime prospects for major gifts. The potential for group gifts is enormous because of the sheer number of these groups, their networking capability, and their ability to pool resources for a larger gift. When several alumni or parents clubs make gifts on an annual basis, the amount can be significant. In pursuing gifts from organizations, it is critical to elicit support from key members within the group who can assume the advocacy role on behalf of the library. Parents clubs are ideal groups for giving because they are very sensitive to the role of the library in furthering their children's education. These groups tend to make gifts to the university annually for student related activities and are very open to library projects. At Texas A&M University, the Mothers' Clubs, known affectionately as the Aggie Moms, have made significant gifts to the Sterling C. Evans Library and have become a strong advocacy group. Although most of the gifts are under $5,000, they add up. In 1988, 33 clubs made gifts totaling nearly $13,000. In previous years, individual clubs have made substantial gifts, the largest of which was a $25,000 gift from the Dallas County A&M Mothers' Club, raised through sales of their popular cookbook, *Hullabaloo in the Kitchen*.

REUNION CLASS

Another group with potential to make a major gift is the graduating class or the reunion class of returning graduates. If the university has an established tradition of class gifts made by graduating classes, the library should contact key students involved in the selection process (such as the class gift committee) and submit projects for consideration. A strong case can be made for a class gift to the library which has literally touched the lives of everyone in the class. The long-term effects of a graduating class gift can not be overemphasized. Each class gift sets an example for the next class. The students of today who actively support the library will become the major donors of tomorrow once their careers are successfully launched. Maintaining contact with this group especially the student leaders is very important. Libraries should also consider alumni groups returning for their class reunions as prospects for a group gift. This type of solicitation must be carefully coordinated with the alumni association whose staff handles reunion activities and gift proposals. The library should also establish key contacts with the class. The class agent or current donors who are members of the class can play a critical role in convincing the class to pledge a gift to the library.

Alumni, class, and parents groups are the obvious prospects for library gifts because of their ties to the institution. However, they are not the only groups. Other organizations with special interest in the fulfillment of certain projects should also be courted. New York University's Bobst Library turned to local labor leaders and their unions when they sought annual support for the Robert F. Wagner Labor Archives. In the first year of the project, the Bobst Library raised $45,000 from New York City's Central Labor Council, the umbrella organization for more than 600 local unions.

BOOK COLLECTORS

Although fundraisers are primarily concerned with donors of cash gifts, book collectors are a category that should not be overlooked. Collections are a valuable and necessary component of any library's development efforts. Getting a desirable collection donated may be far less expensive than trying to acquire the materials by purchasing them. Gift collections, however, may have hidden costs. Frequently, they require additional resources for preserving, housing, and expanding the collection. When it is evident that donated collections will require financial support, libraries should consider soliciting the donor of the collection (or the donor's family, friends, or business) for a gift to support the collection.

FACULTY AND STAFF

The university community itself may be fertile ground for prospective donors. Current faculty and staff are likely to give more modest gifts, but retired faculty and staff who were habitual users or frequenters of the library are prospects for major gifts, particularly planned gifts. Only recently Duke University's Perkins Library announced a bequest of $380,000 made by a retired librarian who had been curator of manuscripts for 33 years. This planned gift was the largest ever made by a university employee at Duke. Former student workers at the library are also good prospects. Texas A&M University's Evans Library was named in the will of a library student worker from the 1940s. More recently, a graduating student worker in the Reference Division, who also served as chairperson of her class's gift committee, arranged for a class gift to the library of $15,000.

SORORITIES AND FRATERNITIES

Many sororities and fraternities hold annual fundraisers, such as Sigma Chi's Derby Day. Each year the group determines the program or activity to which the funds will be donated. The library is a perfect prospect for such a gift. Moreover, the library may be able to secure a pledge from the group for a three- to five-year commitment. One group can serve as a catalyst for gifts from other fraternities and sororities. With so many sororities and fraternities on campus, the potential for ongoing gifts is enormous.

FRIENDS OF THE LIBRARY

Since current donors are the best prospects for future gifts, members in the Friends of the Library should not be overlooked. Despite their loyalty, not every friends member is a candidate for a major gift, but careful research is bound to reveal at least a few major donor prospects. Since these donors are already accustomed to making annual gifts to the library, they may be able and willing to increase their annual gift. An annual friends membership gift of $1,000 a year over a five- or ten-year period becomes a significant gift that may be relatively easy for some friends to make, especially if spurred on by the incentive of a capital campaign.

MAVERICK DONORS

One other donor category should be mentioned, although the chances of encountering one are remote: the maverick. This donor is exceedingly elusive, yet every library fantasizes about securing one. Maverick donors are capable of making megagifts that appeal to their imagination and fulfill their visions. Their gifts are likely to be project or collections oriented, rather than endowment oriented because they like to see tangible and immediate results. Maverick donors have no particular affiliation with the institution to which they give other than the lure of a particular project or need. They are usually widely recognized for their philanthropy on the regional or national level. Andrew Carnegie and John D. Rockefeller are prototypes. The "Millionaire" of the 1950s television series whose largesse rescued desperate individuals from disaster is a fictional example. More recently, the outspoken Texas billionaire Ross Perot, who supports visionary causes that fire his imagination, has come to epitomize the maverick donor.

DONOR SOLICITATION STRATEGIES

Strategies for reaching donors are as varied as the donors and the projects to which they give. One fundraiser compared the solicitation process to house painting, in that much of the work is in the preparation for the job rather than in the job itself.[7] Developing the right strategy for a particular donor, however, is the critical first step toward getting the gift. The emphasis should always be placed on the donor. The gift requested should be compatible with the donor's interests, and the strategy should be compatible with the donor's decision-making style. Matching the right gift to the right donor using the right approach is one of the secrets to successful fundraising. Familiarity with the donor's background and patterns of giving is essential. Therefore, every solicitation strategy begins with prospect research in an effort to learn everything relevant about the donor. Typically this is handled by the institution's development office. One of the distinct advantages of fundraising for libraries is that the information-searching tools for prospect research are available in-house.

SELECTING THE PROJECT
Selecting the right kind of project for the prospective donor is part of the process. Donors to libraries today generally support five distinct areas:

- Collections
- Bricks and mortar
- Endowed chairs/curatorships
- Preservation
- Technology

Preservation and technology are newer areas; nevertheless, they are garnering a growing share of interest and support. Knowing which area has the greatest appeal to a particular donor is central to developing a strategy for the solicitation.

INDIVIDUAL SOLICITATION

Prescribed strategies for soliciting donors are included in the most basic texts and guides on fundraising. Personal or one-on-one solicitation is a given. For important gifts, the individual must be solicited in person either with or without a written proposal, depending on the situation. It is possible to get a $1,000 or even a $5,000 gift by writing a personalized and convincing appeal or through a presentation to a group, but beyond that point someone will have to visit with the individuals and ask outright. Everything about the solicitation visit should be thought out well in advance. The site for the solicitation (office, home, library, club, etc.) may vary, but it is always an important consideration. Who will visit the prospect is the key factor in the strategy. The solicitor(s) may vary, but it should always be the person or persons most trusted and respected by the prospective donor and most able to make a compelling case for the library's proposal. More often than not, it will be the library director. In the case of six-figure gifts, it may well require the institution's president or the vice-president for development, as well. Peer solicitation, one donor asking a prospect at his own level, used to be the order of the day. It works, especially if the peer is accompanied by the library director or the president, but it is by no means the only way. Most prospective donors want to hear from the person most able to justify the request and most knowledgeable about the organization to which they are asked to give.

GROUP SOLICITATION

Gifts from a group are handled somewhat differently. The request may not be as specific or direct and is more likely to take the form of a presentation at a meeting of the targeted group or a proposal letter. In other instances it may be more effective to invite the group to the library for a tour and/or demonstration related to the project for which the funds are requested. Regardless of the technique employed, the more prospective donors see and understand about the library the more likely they are to give. Groups such as alumni clubs and parents clubs often hold their own fundraising events for special projects such as scholarships. Once the library has established a strong relationship with a particular group, the library director or the development officer should ask the group to host an annual fundraiser. The San Antonio alumni organization for Texas A&M University (San Antonio A&M Club) holds a casino night each year for the University's Evans Library with annual proceeds averaging $2,000.

A major factor in the solicitation strategy is knowing what type of gift appeals to the donor and the form in which the gift may most easily be made. Some donors are able to make a large cash gift, while other donors prefer installments. Others may prefer to make the gift in the form of stocks and securities, or real estate. Older donors may be candidates for deferred giving in the form of a bequest or planned gift. Good donor prospect research will alert the library to the form of giving best for the donor.

TYPES OF GIFTS

Selecting the type of gift that meets both the library's needs and the donor's preference requires ingenuity and flexibility on the library's part. Institutions and libraries prefer the unrestricted gift which can be spent now as the library sees fit or placed in an endowment or trust fund where the income accrues for use later. Large gifts of this kind are sometimes hard to acquire because they are vague and abstract and nonparticipatory. Donors prefer tangible projects such as collections, services, preservation, construction, and renovation. To appeal to donors, the library must show how endowment gifts will meet tangible needs and goals.

ENDOWED BOOK FUNDS

One program to support collections that has demonstrated donor appeal is the Stanford University Libraries endowed book funds program. Begun over 90 years ago, the program seeks endowments of $10,000 and above for collection support. Donors get their own uniquely designed bookplate in the subject area of their choice. The Stanford Libraries now have over 150 endowed book funds ranging in size from $10,000 to more than $500,000. Many donors increase their bookfunds over time. To recognize these donors and to publicize the program, Stanford produces an attractive brochure with biographical sketches of the donors and reproductions of their bookplates.

ELECTRONIC INFORMATION SOURCES

Although the lure of gifts to support collections has traditionally been strong, donors are beginning to recognize the library's expanding role in providing electronic information services. Libraries that emphasize electronic access as part of their fundraising strategy have spawned a new breed of supporters: technology donors. Typically these donors have engineering or business backgrounds and respond to appeals for equipment that gives access to the online catalog, such as computers and printers. These items are relatively inexpensive gifts and offer visible recognition when the equipment bears a donor plate.

Texas A&M's Evans Library has seen rapid growth in the number of technology donors over the past three years, largely because of extensive publicity and demonstrations of database searching that have been given to targeted groups and individuals. The alumni association, spurred on by its president, an enthusiastic user of electronic databases, recently committed $40,000 a year to fund online database searches for students. Another donor and his wife, excited about providing information to students using databases on CD-ROM, donated $200,000 to create a laser disk searching service with multiple work stations. Most recently ARCO Chemical Company made a $50,000 gift for database searching of business, science, and engineering indexes with document delivery to faculty in their offices and labs via telefacsimile. Subscriptions to databases has become a very popular gift item. Groups such as parents clubs, graduating classes, alumni clubs, and the friends are ideal prospects. Part of the appeal of technology gifts is recognition—the donor's name can be programmed in to appear on the screen or on a printout.

MOTIVATIONS FOR GIVING

Major donors to all types of charitable causes are often asked what motivated them to give. Indeed much has been written on the subject where donors have very willingly explained the impetus and the rationale for a particular gift. Panas's *Mega Gifts* is filled with such accounts. This information can be found not only in texts on fundraising but closer to home in library newsletters. To succeed at fundraising it is essential to understand donors' motives.

In his text on fundraising, Harold Seymour offers two funda-mental observations about donor motivation:

1. Donors must be asked to make a major gift, and they must be asked by someone whom they respect at their own level or higher.
2. Donors respond emotionally and then rationalize their reasons for the gift afterwards.

When these two factors are taken into account in planning a solicitation, the result can be a gift that is far larger than what the donor might originally have anticipated.[8]

The human need to give, like the need for love, is a powerful, innate motivation. In *The Art of Asking*, Schneiter notes that even charitable acts are not totally selfless. In the psychology of giving, he believes donors are motivated to give for seven fundamental reasons:

1. For religious reasons out of a desire for spiritual and earthly rewards.
2. Out of a sense of guilt and the need for atonement.
3. Out of a desire for recognition to secure immortality through good deeds.
4. Out of fear and the desire for self-preservation.
5. For tax benefits, though this is a secondary motivation.
6. Out of a sense of obligation or indebtedness for favors or services.
7. In response to the pressures of a powerful appeal.[9]

The legendary megadonors do not give merely because of need. Although they are reasonably sympathetic and responsive, they do not give to causes in pathetic or desperate straits. They give to fulfill visions and dreams, and they give to heroic causes, according to Panas in *Mega Gifts*.[10] They like bold imaginative projects, and they shun the pedestrian and mundane.

THE PSYCHOLOGY OF DONORS

The psychology of donors is fairly simple; they give because it makes them feel good and because the cause is both important and worthy of their attention. They give to build strengths rather than to shore up weaknesses. They look for potential in a cause where their commitment can make a difference. Donors are motivated by worthy, winning causes. The appeal of such a cause has all the aura of a romance. Donors view their gifts as investments in the future of an institution or organization. Although many are risk takers, they take calculated risks. They will not risk a poor investment in the name of charity or philanthropy.

Donors make their decisions about large gifts, not just on the basis of the project itself and its cost, but on the thinking behind it and the way in which it is presented. Few donors are impressed by fancy packaging and flashy brochures. Major donors prefer the unadorned, well-written, individualized proposal to the glitz of an image-oriented brochure. An effective, well-reasoned presentation is expensive in time and personnel, not in materials. In the end clear and honest communication with a donor will reap long-term dividends.

Many donors are attracted to worthy causes that they feel have been neglected. Academic libraries fall into this niche. Donors to the library often express their concern that support for the library has been subordinated to other areas. Within the university, the competition for donor attention is keen and necessitates coordination of solicitation efforts by the central development office. The need to support endowed chairs, scholarships, research projects, and athletics may be more widely publicized and more glamourized than the need to support the library. In addition many of these gifts, such as endowed chairs feature name recognition for the donors. With such a cornucopia of opportunities vying for their attention, most library donors are not only sensitive to the library's lack of visibility, they are eager to rectify it. They view their own gift as a catalyst for other gifts and take it upon themselves to proselytize about the library. Thus, this "underdog" or "stepchild" image is one that savvy library administrators should exploit to the fullest advantage in their fundraising.

DONOR RECOGNITION

Academic libraries with established development programs have donor relations programs, but the concept may be completely foreign to libraries just launching their fundraising efforts. Donor relations encompasses two components: solicitation and recognition. The significance of solicitation is fairly obvious; you must ask if you want to receive. The importance of recognition, however, is too often overlooked. The means by which the library expresses appreciation to donors is every bit as important as receiving the gift. Recognition is one of the vital factors in wooing and winning donors and in encouraging them to make future gifts. Prospective donors will rarely initiate a discussion about how the gift will be recognized; yet it is very important to their sense of pride and accomplishment. A donor should never have to ask about recognition. Out of a sense of decorum most donors will say that it is unnecessary because the pleasure is in the giving of the gift rather than in its recognition. Nevertheless, the library's responsibility is not only to confer recognition in a manner befitting the donor and the gift, but to discuss it in a tasteful, sensitive way during the solicitation.

RECOGNITION PROGRAMS

It is also the responsibility of the library to institute some kind of recognition program as part of its development efforts. Many academic libraries rely on the university's donor recognition program, if such a program is already in place. This recognition may lead to future gifts to the university, but not necessarily to the library. It is to the library's advantage to have its own donor recognition program because it establishes a closer relationship with the donor which can lead to future gifts and it allows the donor to be thanked by both the university and the library.

A donor recognition program consists of several established methods of expressing appreciation. In listing his principles for successful fundraising, Panas advocates practicing the "rule of sevens," by which a donor should be thanked seven ways for a gift.[11] This tenet, by which he swears, can easily be incorporated in the design of any recognition program. The following are basic components of a donor recognition program for major gifts:

1. Prompt and gracious acknowledgment of the gift by the library director, the vice president for development, and the president.
2. Appropriate publicity in library newsletter, development office newsletter, alumni newsletter, and others.
3. Luncheon, ceremony, reception, or other special event honoring the donor.
4. Memento marking the occasion and inscription of donor's name on the library's recognition plaque or artwork.
5. Follow-up visits, briefings, or reports on the project as appropriate.

The plan described above includes ample opportunity to thank the donor at least seven times and paves the way for future solicitations.

STEWARDSHIP

Stewardship, a term often used in conjunction with donor relations, encompasses the entire cycle of fundraising. It is a philosophical approach to development which promotes long-term relationships with donors through "identification (including research), cultivation, solicitation, recognition, and finally, looking after the gift."[12] As in the biblical parable of the faithful servant, the good steward receives a just reward. Contact with previous donors is just as important as contact with current donors. There is an old saying among fundraisers that if you take care of thanking all the donors, the rest will take care of itself.

One of the most effective ways of thanking donors is to honor them with an award for a truly unique or outstanding gift. Library awards for philanthropy are made on the national, state, and local levels. The library should consider nominating its donors for such awards. Library benefactor awards engender goodwill and donor loyalty. They also assure future gifts. The thrill for the donor is immeasurable, and the award offers additional opportunities to publicize the gift and thank the donor in an even more public way.

CONCLUSION

The focus of a library's development program should be on the giver, as well as the gift. The library must have an effective way not only of identifying and soliciting donor prospects, but recognizing them as well. Donors who feel appreciated give again and encourage others to give. The word spreads quickly when donors are treated with thoughtfulness as though their friendship were valued as much as their gift. Above every library development or administrative office should be emblazoned: Ask not what the donor can do for the library, ask what the library can do for the donor.

Every library that lives by that rule is assured of success in its fundraising.

ENDNOTES

1. Harold J. Seymour, *Designs for Fund Raising*, (New York: McGraw-Hill, 1966), ix.
2. Kent E. Dove, "Donors: Who and Why," National Society for Fund Raising Executives, San Antonio Chapter's Fund Raising '89 Conference, February 10, 1989.
3. Debbie Goldberg, "How the Other Half Gives," *Currents* XV, 3   4. Goldberg, 11.
5. Goldberg, 11.
6. Jerold Panas, *Mega Gifts* (Chicago: Pluribus Press), 21.
7. Paul H. Schneiter, *The Art of Asking,* (New York: Walker and Company), 33.
8. Seymour, 29.
9. Schneiter, 23-29.
10. Panas, 66.
11. Panas, 187
12. Deborah Hopkinson, "Thanks for Everything," *Currents*, XV, 5 (May 1989): 55.

4 GRANTS

by Helen W. Samuels

Samuel A. Streit

Academic research libraries have increased their reliance on grant funding over the past 20 years. Both public and private sources have, with varying degrees of generosity, played a major role as academic libraries have grappled with issues as varied as automated bibliographic control, materials acquisitions, preservation, and capital projects. Given the one factor common to all such library endeavors, their large and ever-increasing cost, grants correctly have been viewed by many in the research library community as one of the most important means for addressing needs and opportunities beyond the routine. This has been especially true for at least a decade, during which time academic institutions have been beset at every turn with rapidly rising costs and proliferating demands upon static, or in many instances, diminishing levels of income from investment, tuition, and public revenues.

As institutions of higher education confront the last decade of the century, the omens for an improved financial picture from traditional sources of income are not encouraging. Indeed, even the grant sources that have been a mainstay for many academic research libraries may be in jeopardy as public agencies are targeted by political conservatives and budgetary authorities and as private foundations reassess their priorities relative to higher education, environmental concerns, elementary and secondary education, and a host of other social issues. As a result, the competition for grant funds within the academic research library community will intensify for the foreseeable future. This chapter is intended to assist academic librarians and development officers who are contending for funds in this increasingly competitive environment.

DEFINING THE PROJECT

Perhaps the most fundamental issue to be faced when contemplating a grant proposal centers upon defining a project that promotes the library's long-term goals. It is not uncommon for libraries to seek grants on the Mount Everest principal—that is, to apply simply because they are there, rather than selectively submitting proposals that address real needs. The library that indiscriminately seeks grant funding, no matter how successful the endeavor, runs the risk of allowing grants to drive its priorities. Indeed, such grants can have a deleterious effect because the library may be required to reallocate scarce human and financial resources in order to carry out the grant project. It is far better to write grant proposals judiciously, as one component of the library's master plan for achieving its goals and devising its development strategies.

With these general principles in mind, a rational approach to grant writing is to focus on discrete, well-defined projects with a prescribed scope and duration that are integral to the library's overall objectives. Typically, these projects can be subsumed within seven broad categories: acquisitions, processing, capital projects, preservation, research and development, programs and outreach, and institutional projects.

ACQUISITIONS

Acquisitions are perhaps the most obvious funding priority for academic research libraries. But despite their importance to both libraries and the scholarly community, many funding agencies do not find acquisitions proposals appealing, the assumption being either that purchasing library materials is a responsibility that should be met by the institution's own budget and/or that acquisitions needs are a bottomless pit which grant funds will do little to fill. Even federal programs with acquisitions as a stated area of interest, distribute relatively little funding for buying library materials. Still, there are public and private foundations that will entertain acquisitions proposals, including the Department of Education's Title II-C Program and such private foundations as Kress and Booth-Ferris, which have made acquisitions grants to academic research libraries in art and international studies respectively. Locally oriented foundations also sometimes fund acquisitions projects but many balk at proposals to benefit a small number of scholars in a specialized field of learning as opposed to addressing the reading needs of the general public. When seeking grant funding for acquisitions it is also important to bear in mind that research libraries often prefer to establish endowments for acquisitions and that many grant sources have policies that preclude giving to endowment for any purpose. This underscores the need to screen potential grant sources carefully to identify those that are likely to fund acquisitions and to tailor the proposal to the funder's requirements.

PROCESSING

The processing of research materials, ranging from the straightforward cataloging of books and serials to the specialized arrangement and description of manuscripts, archives, photographs, art properties, and sound recordings in their numerous formats, has been a long-term area of grant activity in academic libraries. The attraction of processing proposals, to libraries and funding sources alike, lies partly in the fact that processing work can be divided into projects of manageable size and duration. Further, for somewhat over a decade the majority of processing proposals have been predicated upon sharing bibliographic information with a vast community of scholars through national and international electronic databases. Through such projects, research libraries are able to make their holdings known in ways hitherto impossible and funding sources realize their goal of bestowing grants that benefit the largest audience possible.

The federal government, through the National Endowment for the Humanities, the DOE Title II-C Program, and the National Historical Publications and Records Commission, has distributed millions of dollars to the research library community for processing projects as have some of the nation's largest private foundations, such as the Mellon Foundation and the Pew Charitable Trusts. In addition, many smaller, often local, foundations have made similar grants on the premise that such projects are a wise investment because they spread information throughout the local community and advertise local cultural resources to a broader audience.

Projects funded by processing grants vary in size from multimillion dollar cataloging and retrospective conversion efforts that make entire library collections accessible to a wider audience, to smaller, narrowly defined projects that make available special collections materials of interest primarily to specialized researchers. Given the rapid rate at which general library materials have been added to the principal national databases over the last decade, the current trend in processing grants appears to give greater emphasis to unique materials that are unlikely to be represented in either online or printed collection guides. There is evidence that some funding sources, both public and private, are losing interest in any kind of processing grant, and the numbers and dollar amounts of such grants are dropping. Regardless of whether such evidence presents a trend, it is apparent that processing grants that make available demonstrably important research collections as opposed to large omnibus proposals that do little more than add local holding symbols to existing bibliographic records will be preferred by funders.

CAPITAL PROJECTS

Libraries frequently seek, with some success, grant funding for capital projects including renovations, expansions, and new construction. It is uncommon for an entire capital project to be funded with grant funds, but frequently a publicly funded government program, notably the NEH challenge grant program, or a private foundation, such as Kresge, will contribute toward a building program. In addition, local foundations which have little general interest in libraries will contribute to a bricks and mortar project. Conventional wisdom has it that donors, including most foundations, respond to new construction more favorably than they do to renovations. New construction generates more enthusiasm (hence more publicity) and there are more possibilities for naming opportunities. While this may be true to some extent, research libraries should not be discouraged from seeking grant funds for renovation projects, particularly if the project involves the restoration of an architecturally distinguished building or has as its purpose the preservation of valuable research materials through improved environmental conditions.

PRESERVATION

In addition to their interest in capital projects that emphasize preservation, research libraries, and some granting sources, are interested in preserving library and archival materials themselves, an interest that has paralleled the steady development of new conservation techniques and the expansion of the preservation profession itself. Both libraries and granting sources have stressed preserving content through surrogate media, microform in particular, rather than artifactual conservation. Consequently, many—and frequently very large—grants have been made to microfilm unique, fragile, and rare materials as well as more mundane deteriorating material of current or potential interest to scholars. Such grants have been awarded by the major federal agencies, by a few state governments, New York being a praiseworthy example, and by private foundations including, for example, the Mellon Foundation.

Printed materials on highly acidic paper have been the chief objectives of preservation grants to date, but manuscripts and archival materials also have benefited. Grants have been made to conserve photographic and audio resources by recopying deteriorating originals. Filming projects remain a high priority with libraries and funding sources, as witnessed by a recent NEH grant to the Research Libraries Group for a multi-institutional manuscript filming grant. Recently, however, more grant funds have been made available for conserving library and archival materials in their original format. Increasing awareness of the importance of original format, the greater availability of skilled conservationists, more sophisticated conservation techniques, and the simple fact that vast amounts of research materials have been filmed, suggest that a shift in funding patterns may be emerging. Indeed, the next wave of preservation grant proposals may very well come in the wake of the mass deacidification process soon to be available through the Library of Congress.

RESEARCH AND DEVELOPMENT

Research and development can be the primary intent of a grant project or a complementary benefit. Some foundations, such as the Council on Library Resources,(CLR) the H W. Wilson Foundation, and the National Historical Publications and Records Commission, frequently make grants that have research and development as their principal objective. These grants often sponsor research on matters of import to the entire library and archival communities, such as acquisitions and pricing trends for research materials, the development of preservation and conservation techniques, or the use of technology that enhances access to specialized library and archival holdings. CLR grants, for example, are awarded to individuals, libraries, and large projects that benefit the entire research library community, the latter typified by the Commission of Preservation and Access and the Linked Systems Project of the Bibliographic Development Program. Also of value to research libraries is the CLR Cooperative Research Grant program which stimulates communication between librarians and academic faculty through joint projects that explore issues of concern to research libraries and their scholar users.

Research can be a productive side effect of almost any project if a deliberate attempt is made to ask questions of the project, to generalize upon project findings and to publish results that can benefit others. In this manner a local grant takes on greater usefulness and meaning, and is clearly more attractive to the funding agency. The key to success for many proposals (including those that have such workaday activities as retrospective conversion as their ultimate objective) lies in demonstrating that the project will produce new information or new approaches or solutions to problems that are shared by many libraries. While granting sources tend to avoid making awards to proposals that are loaded with gimmicks or which make groundless claims of importance, they often do favor proposals that not only have practical ends but that also employ creative methods and strategies in their implementation.

PROGRAMS AND OUTREACH

Programmatic grants, especially those that focus on outreach or public relations, continue to be a major funding priority of research libraries. Typical program grants sought by academic research libraries support exhibitions, many of which are accompanied by scholarly catalogs; conferences and symposia, frequently conducted in conjunction with academic faculty, that are based upon the library's exceptional subject strengths and that address topics and issues of interest to a broad scholarly audience; and programs that may or may not complement the library's strengths, but which have a strong popular appeal to the entire campus community and to the general public.

Major exhibitions and scholarly conferences are often successful in attracting grant funds from public agencies, in particular from the NEH and its state humanities council counterparts. Private foundations also sponsor this sort of activity, although locally based foundations may tend to prefer programs that have a wide, general appeal to those that are of interest to a relatively few academicians. An excellent example of a private foundation grant that combined a major exhibition, a scholarly conference, and engendered wide public enthusiasm was that awarded by the Pew Charitable Trusts to the Philadelphia Area Consortium of Special Collections Libraries (PACSCL) for its 1988 Legacies of Genius exhibition and accompanying series of programs. Designed to display the treasures of the 16 member libraries within the context of their research potential, the exhibition, scholarly conference, and numerous programs intended for a nonscholarly audience were a resounding success and served as the basis for additional cooperative projects.

INTERINSTITUTIONAL PROJECTS

Many large and successful grant projects that support academic research libraries are interinstitutional in nature. Some, like the PACSCL project, include strong research collections in nonacademic institutions and in smaller academic libraries as well as those located in major academic research libraries; the common binding factor in such projects usually is either a shared locality or a shared subject strength. Other interinstitutional projects may be scattered geographically, the physical separation being bridged electronically. The numerous grants awarded by the principal federal agencies, and by nationally oriented private foundations, attest to the appeal that such proposals can generate. For example, member institutions of the Research Libraries Group have received large multiyear grants from NEH and from the Mellon Foundation to support RLG's preservation microfilming projects and such major bibliographic efforts as the automated Archives and Manuscripts Control (AMC) program and several retrospective conversion projects. RLG cooperative retrospective conversion projects also have received major assistance from the Hewlett and Getty Foundations.

Consortial grants have the advantage of appealing to the granting source's desire to see its funds benefit large segments of the population. They also are attractive to both grantor and grantee because the project's product is greater than the sum of its individual, institutional parts. In addition, a single, primary grantee acting on behalf of a number of institutions facilitates grant administration. Consortial grants provide a mechanism for shared problem solving when administering a grant. Of course, consortial grants have disadvantages as well as advantages. The need to compromise on the size of the project components, the amount of support that each institution receives, and the practical difficulties involved in coordinating the various grant components relative to timing and maintaining the overall project schedule are among the most common difficulties. On balance, however, many academic research libraries strongly believe that the advantages considerably outweigh the disadvantages with the result that consortial grants have become an important component in their overall fundraising efforts.

GOVERNMENT GRANTS

Competition for government grants is intense since few agencies support library activities, and cuts in the federal budget mean fewer dollars to go around. The bulk of the funds are made available by three agencies: the Department of Education (DOE), the National Endowment for the Humanities (NEH), and the National Historical Publications and Records Commission (NHPRC).

The emphasis in the following sections is on federal funds. State and local governments also make funds available to libraries and archives through their humanities and cultural councils or other agencies. As these programs differ greatly, inquiries should be made through state and local government offices to determine their availability. The application procedure described at the end of this chapter, however, will probably serve for state and local, as well as federal government grants.

The most comprehensive source of information about federal grant and benefit programs is the *Catalog of Federal Domestic Assistance* issued by OMB and GSA and available through the GPO. This publication provides information about 1,100 grant, loan, and benefit programs administered by 52 agencies. The publication is issued annually in paper form and is also distributed as an automated database. It has a subject index that includes terms such as libraries. Information on specific federal funding programs is available from the relevant government agencies; request copies of their guidelines. Institutions can be placed on mailing lists to receive updated copies of the guidelines each year.

TITLE II

The Title II—College and Research Library Assistance and Library Training and Research programs of the Department of Education were established to help institutions of higher education acquire materials, establish and maintain networks for sharing library resources, train librarians, and maintain, strengthen, and share collections. The Office of Education Research and Improvement of DOE administers several programs, generally referred to by their letter designations and titles. Comprehending the goals of these individual programs and the types of projects that are funded can, however, be a bit of a challenge. Published guidelines are available for each program, but on the whole the brochures are reprints of the Federal Register text with little additional explanation or clarification. The goals of some of the programs overlap, creating additional confusion. A small staff administers this program, and, unlike NEH and NHPRC, they are generally not able to review and guide grant applications before they are submitted. It is therefore necessary to read the brochures carefully, and when possible to talk with colleagues who have been awarded grants and read their proposals. Following are brief descriptions of the primary programs likely to be of interest to academic libraries.

Title II, Part B: Library Career Training Program—Fellowships and Institutes: Institutions of higher education and library organizations are eligible to apply for fellowship funds to train librarians, and especially to provide training to meet the challenges

of new techniques and technologies, and increase the excellence of library education. Funds are generally awarded to schools of library science and to professional organizations.

Title II, Part B: Library Research and Demonstration Program: This program encourages research, development and demonstration activities that improve libraries through:

1. The promotion of economical and efficient delivery of information
2. Cooperative efforts
3. Developmental projects
4. The improvement of information technology
5. Training in librarianship
6. The dissemination of information derived from these projects

For example, funds have been given to Baruch College to demonstrate the benefits of hypermedia to teach students how to do research, to Rutgers University to study the use of online information services, and to the University of Wisconsin—Madison to develop a method to evaluate adult literacy programs.

Title II, Part C: Strengthening Research Library Resources Program: Title II-C is probably the most familiar to the library community, and has probably made the greatest impact on research libraries as a source of support for their collections. The purpose of the program is to promote research and education of high quality throughout the United States by providing financial assistance to the nation's major libraries; to strengthen and preserve their collections and make their holdings available to other libraries. The objectives are to enhance the national bibliographic database by adapting, converting or creating library records for unique materials, to augment and preserve unique collections, and to promote the sharing of library resources. The specific list of activities that are eligible for support include: acquisition of library materials; preservation of library materials including microfilming, binding, rebinding, and photocopying; cataloging and the preparation of guides to collections (including the arrangement and description of manuscript collections); and sharing of library material by mail, electronic or conventional means. Title II-C provides funds to acquire the equipment and staff to make these activities possible.

To be eligible to apply for these funds an institution must have a major research library holding significant collections that support scholarly research by individuals at their own institution and outside researchers as well. For this reason, the Title II-C application has two parts. The first portion requests information about the institution and its library, while the second specifically describes the proposed project. If review of the first part of the application affirms that the institution meets the criteria as a major research library, they are then eligible for Title II-C grants for the next four years.

Over the years the clear emphasis of Title II-C funding has been in the area of bibliographic control. Libraries have used these funds to catalog unique material for the first time, and even more to re-catalog items ("recon" projects) and enter new records into the national bibliographic databases. Bibliographic control projects clearly support the program's objects to share information and collections. It is often harder to justify funds for acquisition and preservation, but these activities are still funded each year.

Title II, Part D: College Library Technology and Cooperation Grants: This program is designed to encourage resource-sharing among libraries through the use of technology and networking. Four types of grants are awarded to help libraries obtain equipment needed to participate in a network, establish facilities and expand programs that improve information services, and conduct research and demonstration projects to enhance library information services. Among the activities supported by Title II-D are, buying access to networks and paying telecommunication charges, and paying for equipment and staff.

Examples of Title IID support include grants to Saint Mary's College of Minnesota to replace their stand-alone automated system with participation in PALS (the Minnesota cooperative automated library system), to the Boston Library Consortium to provide electronic access to the Consortium's Union List of Serials, and to the University of California—Berkeley to develop automated search strategies to remedy the problem of retrieving too much or too little information from online library catalogs.

NATIONAL ENDOWMENT FOR THE HUMANITIES
The National Endowment for the Humanities provides support to libraries through their Division of Research Programs, the Office of Preservation, and their challenge grant program. NEH's goal is to encourage scholarship in the humanities, and their library programs therefore aim to increase the availability of important research collections and preserve them.

The Reference Materials program of NEH's Division of Research provides funds to libraries and archives through their Access category. The types of projects they support include:

- Researching developments affecting the availability of information
- Arranging and describing significant archival and manuscript collections
- Surveys to locate significant archival materials
- Arranging, describing, and preserving graphic, film, sound, and artifact collections
- Preparing microfilm copies of unique materials
- Microfilming unique collections in foreign repositories to make them available in this country
- Preparing bibliographies to facilitate research in areas of the humanities
- Cataloging significant collections of printed works
- Cataloging manuscripts dating before 1600
- Preparing indices to significant research materials
- Conducting oral histories designed to supplement strong documentary collections
- Preparing other scholarly finding aids to facilitate use of resources by researchers.

The Office of Preservation was established to address the problem of the rapid physical deterioration of books, manuscripts, photographs, sound recordings, films and other research materials. The Office not only supports efforts to preserve these resources, but also the education of preservation personnel, the establishment and operation of regional preservation services, research to improve preservation technology and procedures, state and regional preservation planning activities, and efforts to improve the public's understanding of these problems. To date, the bulk of the funds have been spent on projects to prepare preservation microfilm copies of brittle and deteriorating books and serials.

NATIONAL HISTORICAL PUBLICATIONS AND RECORDS COMMISSION

Finally, the National Historical Publications and Records Commission, a unit within the National Archives, supports activities relating to the preservation, publication and use of documentary sources relating to the history of the United States. NHPRC's Records Program funds projects that: improve programs of public and private organizations designed to preserve archival collections; conduct research aimed at improving recordkeeping techniques; educate and train archivists and records custodians; establish new institutional records programs; arrange, describe and preserve significant collections of historical records; prepare multi-institutional guides and databases describing historical records; and conduct surveys to locate records not in repositories. NHPRC also funds feasibility and consulting grants to explore major projects and advise institutions seeking assistance. Commission funds have been a particularly important source for colleges and universities seeking to establish new archival and records management programs at their institutions.

PRIVATE FOUNDATION GRANTS

As with public funding agencies, private foundations have giving profiles that determine such matters as whether they will accept proposals from academic libraries, the size of grants, funding priorities, and such idiosyncratic considerations as geographic or sectarian restrictions, willingness to support endowment, predilections toward challenge grants, etc. Nationally oriented foundations, such as the Mellon, Pew, Hewlett, and Getty Foundations, frequently prefer innovative projects that can serve as models or that will be of national significance in some other way. Conversely, locally oriented foundations, including many associated with businesses or corporations, emphasize projects that will have a strong impact upon the immediate geographical area and its inhabitants. Many foundations, though not all by any means, will fund only those proposals that in some way reflect the interests of the donor, interests that may be determined by the wishes of an individuals or of a corporation which makes grants in areas of concern to the company itself. Other foundations support only certain types of projects, such as construction, programs, outreach, etc.

GUIDES TO PRIVATE FOUNDATIONS

Identifying private foundations need not be a complicated process if the library goes about the task systematically and realistically. There are several published guides that provide information on areas of interest to foundations, their location, instructions for application, even the academic affiliations of the principals responsible for deciding awards; often idiosyncratic information is included also, such as geographic or sectarian restrictions, willingness or unwillingness to support endowment, etc. Perhaps the best known information source for identifying foundations is the Foundation Center and in particular its three published and frequently updated guides, *The Foundation Directory*, *Source Book Profiles*, and *Foundation Grants Index*. The *Directory* offers succinct information on some 5,000 foundations with assets of at least $1,000,000 or which award a total of $100,000 or more annually; the *Source Book* provides more comprehensive information on approximately 1,000 of the largest foundations while the *Index*, which is issued bi-monthly, offers information on recent grants of $5,000 or more awarded by the larger foundations. The Foundation Center also maintains a file of IRS 990 Private Foundation forms, a valuable source of information for identifying smaller foundations that may not be listed in the *Directory*. These forms are available at most of the Center's cooperating libraries or copies can be ordered through a fee-based telephone reference service.

PROFESSIONAL LITERATURE

The Taft Group also offers guides and directories similar to those available from the Foundation Center. Perhaps the most useful Taft publications are the *Taft Foundation Giving Directory*, the *Taft Foundation Reporter*, and a newsletter, the *Foundation Giving Watch*. The *Giving Watch* is useful for its updating on trends and news in philanthropy, and its list of foundations by focus or geographical area. The Gale Research Company also publishes directories and guides to philanthropy, a particularly useful title being the *International Foundation Directory* which provides an overview to giving by foreign foundations.

Grant sources often can be identified by reading library professional literature and the "trade" journals of higher education and fundraising. The eleven annual issues of *College and Research Libraries News*, a publication of the Association of College and Research Libraries/American Library Association, carry announcements and brief descriptions of grants to academic libraries as do the *Chronicle of Higher Education* and its subsidiary publication, the *Chronicle of Philanthropy*.

Now in its second year of publication, the *Chronicle of Philanthropy* is a particularly useful tool, not only for identifying grant sources, but for its incisive overview of the entire field of philanthropic giving. Each issue contains an array of articles on a broad range of topics pertaining to philanthropy at every level and from every identifiable source. It contains a new grants column, a "people" column that includes foundation staff changes and new foundation board members. There are also book reviews, and a legislative update, which is quite useful as it relates to changing regulations for sources of public funding.

ONLINE SOURCES

Online sources are becoming increasingly useful in researching foundations. Virtually all academic research libraries subscribe to the DIALOG Information Service through which the Foundation Center's databases are available. Information in these files conforms to that found in the Center's publications but has the obvious advantage of being more current. DIALOG also now provides several full text files of documents such as press releases, interviews, and articles pertaining to foundations. Online databases allow the researcher to manipulate information to meet specific requirements, such as compiling a list of foundations that support academic libraries in a given region, and allows the information either to be downloaded or printed off-line and mailed. If the development officer does not have the requisite equipment or training for online searching, the library reference staff frequently will provide, at cost, needed access to a relevant database. Indeed, if the development officer is working on behalf of the library, it is quite possible that the library will absorb the connect charges and user fees.

CLEARANCE

Regardless of the nature of a grant proposal or the funding source to which it is to be submitted, there are several fundamental preliminary matters that the astute grant writer must address: the first of these is clearance, or permission to move ahead with a proposal. Within an academic research library, clearance usually means securing approval of the library's senior administration and it may involve negotiating with other units of the library which are competing either for grant funds, or for staff and equipment needed to implement a successful grant proposal. Frequently, all potential grant proposals are required to be coordinated with the university's central development office and/or the senior administration of the institution. This may be true even in universities with highly decentralized development structures wherein various professional schools have their own development offices.

The coordination between the library and its parent entity consists of receiving permission to move forward with a proposal. It also may involve directives as to which funding sources may, or may not, be approached and who is permitted to make the contact. The university often rigorously controls which of its many components may approach a given funding source and woe betide the hapless library fundraiser who applies to a foundation earmarked for the medical school! This sort of difficulty can only be avoided through close coordination of the library's fundraising priorities and preliminary strategies with those of the parent institution. The library may not always be pleased with the position that it occupies in the university's funding hierarchy, but to blunder along without consultation may have far worse consequences.

THE PROPOSAL

WHO SHOULD WRITE IT?

An important preliminary to consider when seeking grants is deciding who will actually write the proposal. Logically, the individual(s) closest to the actual project to be undertaken should take the leading role in constructing the proposal. Depending upon the nature of the project, librarians from many parts of the organization may be involved, but for best results it is preferable to have a single individual responsible for coordinating the various components of the proposal and imposing upon it a single stylistic and editorial hand.

Also in those universities where grants are generated in the central development office, it is essential that the library be kept informed of proposals that are being considered and that the librarians be involved in composing the proposals. It is not unheard of for librarians to discover to their dismay that inappropriate proposals have been submitted or that worthwhile opportunities have been botched by a poorly conceived proposal written without input from the library.

WRITING A SUCCESSFUL PROPOSAL

Writing a grant proposal for the first time can be a daunting proposition. Grant writing workshops, offered frequently at library and archival professional meetings, are a way to learn the ropes and gain some confidence. It is often more effective, however, to read examples of successful grant applications. Funded grant applications are public documents and should be available from the funding agency or the institution receiving the award. Studying funded proposals reveals not only how a successful application is constructed, but also confirms the type of projects the agency chooses to fund. In addition, accepting the opportunity to review grant applications for a federal agency provides an excellent opportunity to examine the application and review process.

The thorough preparation of a grant proposal can take many months, as project planning and consultation with the grant agency and the institution must precede writing and submission. The application process should start by obtaining a current version of the funding guidelines, and whenever possible contacting the agency to discuss the proposed project. Most foundations and government agencies encourage these early discussions, and therefore regard unannounced applications with great disfavor. Prior discussions and careful review of the guidelines are required to assure that the applicant is proposing a suitable project. It is a great waste of time to submit an application only to learn that the agency or foundation does not fund such projects.

The keys to a good grant application are to give the funders all the information they request, (not more, not less), in the form they request it, to assume nothing, and to use clear language that avoids jargon. The guidelines for the preparation of proposals issued by each funder must be followed closely. A sure way to have a grant rejected is simply not to follow their instructions.

PROPOSAL STYLE

As a general rule the applications submitted to government agencies and to private foundations differ greatly. The style of each foundation differs, but usually they request much less information than the government. A summary description of the project and a detailed budget may suffice. Some foundations permit applicants to structure their own proposals while others provide forms. Check with the foundation grants officers both to review the proposed project and to determine the amount and form of information they require.

REVIEW AND AWARD PROCESS

Applicants should also be aware that the review and award process used by the foundations is much simpler, and usually less time consuming than the government process. Foundations generally rely on their own staff to review proposals and make funding recommendations, while government agencies use a combination of their own staff, external reviewers, expert panels, and administrative review.

WRITING GOVERNMENT PROPOSALS

Government applications demand considerable information, and care must be taken to include all items required, and when specified, in the order requested. For instance, do not assume that everyone knows how you catalog a book, or arrange and describe a manuscript collection, or that the fruits of the work will be properly publicized. All components in the project and all procedures should be explained in detail when appropriate, or at least discussed briefly with proper reference to the standards that will be used to guide the work. On the other hand, padded applications that are overly long and burdened with unnecessary appendices are looked on with disfavor by reviewers and agency staff.

PROPOSAL COMPONENTS

COVER SHEET AND SUMMARY

Government agencies require a cover sheet that includes basic information about the institution submitting the applications and the proposed project. As part of this page or as a separate sheet the applicant is asked to write a summary statement about their proposal. Take care to make this statement clear and complete because it is used both during the review process, and if funded, to publicize the award. NHPRC, for instance, requests the preparation of a two page summary that includes information about the project's purpose and goals, significance, plan of work, products, and key personnel.

NATURE OF THE PROJECT

Applicants must fully describe the nature and objectives of the project, and justify the significance of the work to the institution requesting funding, and when appropriate, to other institutions, scholars and professional communities. Justifications can be based on the significance of the materials to be cataloged, or processed, or the value of the project's findings to other institutions. When appropriate, narrative information can include a history of the project to date, and a description of how the work will continue after the funding ceases. The application should also discuss why outside funds are required, and how this support relates to ongoing institutional support of the program.

INSTITUTIONAL CONTEXT

Applications generally specify some information about the repository (library, archives, or museum) requesting support, and also about their parent institution. Emphasis should be placed on demonstrating the strength of the existing programs, the presence of appropriate resources and the commitment to support the proposed project once the outside funding has ceased.

PROJECT PERSONNEL

Information about personnel must generally be included in two places in the proposal. The narrative portion contains an explanation of the use of staff—both the allocation of time from existing personnel and the desired skills sought in the staff to be hired with grant support. The applicant must demonstrate that the existing personnel are qualified to oversee and carry out this work. The appendices to the application must include curriculum vitae of the principal staff (project director, etc.) and job descriptions for any personnel to be hired.

METHODOLOGY, TECHNIQUES, PLAN OF WORK

These sections describe the specific procedures, standards, techniques, and methods that are to be used. For preservation microfilming, for instance, specifics should be included about the configuration of the images on the film, the target information, the standards used to process the microfilm, the production and storage of negatives, and the distribution of use copies. For cataloging and conversion projects, information about cataloging standards and the use of national library databases should be included. For projects that require automation technology, particular care should be taken to justify the use of the technology chosen, describe the system chosen or the design of the database, and describe how the system will be maintained and updated.

Of particular importance is the detailed plan of work with a chronology of tasks to be accomplished and estimates of personnel needs at each stage. A cursory plan gives the impression that the applicants have not adequately thought out the work required to accomplish their goals. A detailed plan assures the funder that realistic benchmarks have been established that can be used to keep the project on track once it is funded. On the other hand, applicants must guard against being unrealistic about the amount of work that can be accomplished in a given period. Overly ambitious projects are often rejected, or if funded, can create serious problems for the grantee.

BUDGET

Funding agencies are generally quite specific about the budget information they require, and often provide detailed forms for the applicants to complete. Follow the directions carefully, and whatever you do, check and recheck the figures. Sloppy math can shed doubts on an otherwise splendid proposal. Budgets should honestly reflect the costs of a project, but should not be padded.

COST SHARING AND MATCHING FUNDS

Applicants should clarify the type of funds sought (matching or outright) in keeping with agency policy on cost sharing and indirect costs. While some agencies award only outright grants, others (such as NEH and NHPRC) give applicants a choice of outright or matching funds, or the agency can decide which to award. In the case of a matching grant, the institution is required to match the funds dollar-for-dollar from private sources.

Another way agencies lessen the cost of projects and seek institutional support is through cost sharing contributions. In this case the institution is asked to demonstrate cash contributions or in-kind contributions in the form of donated services that will be used to support the project. Agencies often establish goals for cost-sharing contributions for specific types of projects. For instance, NEH's Access program generally seeks a cost-sharing contribution of 20 percent, but when a project focuses on the collections of a specific institution, a 50 percent cost-sharing is required.

Agencies also vary in their willingness to pay indirect costs. Each academic institution works with the government to calculate a recovery rate to pay those costs that are not directly attributed to a specific project. While the salaries and equipment for a project are direct costs, funds for the heating and maintenance of the buildings in which the project is housed and the general administrative costs of running the institution are reflected in the indirect costs. Libraries and other units on academic campuses must request indirect costs if the institution insists, but the agencies might choose not to grant these costs. Then the library must negotiate with the parent institution to determine if the award can still be accepted.

If an application is unsuccessful, most agencies are willing to provide comments based on the reviews and their deliberations. When encouraged to do so, applications should be modified in accordance with the suggestions and resubmitted.

GRANT IMPLEMENTATION

REPORTS

If an application is successful, the work commences: hire staff, purchase equipment, and initiate the plan of work. Granting agencies, government and private foundations, have specific requirements for reporting the progress of work throughout the project. While the government may require a report every six months, a foundation might expect a report only at the end of the funded period. The unit that actually administers the project generally is responsible for the narrative reports, while the financial office of the parent institution prepares the final accounting reports.

COMMUNICATION WITH THE AGENCY OR FOUNDATION

In addition to these formal reports it is important to stay in touch with the granting agency especially when adjustments must be made in the project. If a project is delayed because suitable personnel cannot be located, notify the agency at once and renegotiate the starting date or the length of the grant. If problems are encountered with the equipment, or tasks are taking longer than expected, discuss these issues immediately with a grants officer and agree on solutions. Grant recipients must try to fulfill all of their commitments, and if it looks like that is not possible, it is best to inform the funder as soon as possible.

PUBLICITY

Once the project is completed and the final report submitted to the funder, the accomplishments of the project should be publicized with proper acknowledgment given to the funding agency. Whenever possible the grantee should find ways to build upon the project and make it useful to other institutions, colleagues, researchers, and the public. Copies of publicity, articles, and other relevant materials should be sent to the funder.

SUMMARY

As long as libraries cannot obtain adequate funds from their parent institution to support all of their programs and initiatives, they must seek outside support. Librarians and archivists must therefore know where to seek those resources and how to apply for them.

RESOURCES

Boss, Richard W. *Grant Money and How to Get It: A Handbook for Librarians*. New York: R.R. Bowker, 1980.

Breivik, Patricia Senn and E. Burr Gibson, eds. *Funding Alternatives for Libraries*. Chicago: American Library Association, 1979.

Carter, Yvonne. "Federal Funding for Research and Demonstrations: One of the Few Games in Town." *The Bottom Line* (4), No. 3:9-11.

Corry, Emmet. *Grants for Libraries: A Guide to Public and Private Funding Programs and Proposal Writing Techniques*. Littleton, CO: Libraries Unlimited, 1982.

Spyers-Duran, Peter. "Revitalizing of Academic Library Programs through Creative Fundraising." *Austerity Management in Research Libraries*. Edited by John F. Harvey and Peter Spyers-Duran, Metuchen, N.J.: Scarecrow Press, 1984.

Streit, Samuel. "All that Glitters: Fundraising for Special Collections in Academic Libraries." *Rare Books and Manuscripts Librarianship*, III (Spring, 1988): 31-41.

5 THE CORPORATE CONNECTION

by Susan P. Jordan

There is a natural connection between the academic library and the corporate entity: the distribution of information. The academic library exists to facilitate this distribution through development, preservation, and access to its research collections for the academic institution and for the community-at-large. The timely and accurate processing of information is critical to the success of corporations—the library, therefore, represents an important resource. Although a number of corporations have established in-house libraries, many need additional materials and services available only from an academic research library. Developing a mutually beneficial relationship between the corporation and the library can have a long-term positive impact on both institutions.

This natural connection was confirmed by Ralph Goettler, President of Goettler Associates, in his 1988 address to the American Library Association: ". . . the corporate connection is essential to the welfare of libraries, especially during this period of governmental conservatism. Conversely, corporate leaders are eager to help provide support for the cultural and educational well-being of their respective communities. Nothing, then, is more natural than a coalition between big business and libraries. Both have similar goals and both receive benefits from such a relationship."

TRENDS IN CORPORATE PHILANTHROPY

In comparing corporate support with support from other philanthropic sources in the United States, the breakdown for 1987/1988 was as follows:

Corporate 23%
Foundations 20%
Individuals 49%
Other 8%

Overall, corporate giving today gets mixed reviews. On the positive side, there has been increasing pressure on the private sector to demonstrate greater social responsibility. This reflects a definite shift in funding from the public to the private sector. On the negative side, mergers, acquisitions, and leveraged buy-outs have consolidated many corporations, resulting in a reduction in corporate contributions since the early 1980s. Now rapid corporate change and tax reform measures are stimulating a trend toward "enlightened self-interest" and "cause-related" marketing: programs in which companies tie contributions to sales or to the specific use of products. This trend is likely to continue, since marketing budgets are bigger than contributions budgets.

Another positive development is the corporate directive of Japanese companies integrate more in the activities of American communities. Corporate contributions from European countries may also be on the rise. However, there is a great diversity of corporate giving among various countries, as well as among corporations in each country. There are also variations in the definition of a corporate contribution and tax law incentives. Cultural and historic differences have a dramatic impact on the concept of charity and contributions. The area of international corporate contributions represents an important opportunity for the academic research library. The library will need to design careful strategies to capitalize on this new area of corporate giving.

Higher education continues to compete with other worthy causes for philanthropic support: health services, religious organizations, social services, the arts, and civic/social/fraternal organizations. Corporate giving in the late 1980s has tended to give priority to highly visible causes: the homeless, healthcare, outreach, and other human service programs. A 1987/1988 survey of 1,100 institutions revealed that corporate giving to education/research in 1988 totalled 37 percent of corporate giving. With the exception of an all-time high in 1985, this percentage has remained relatively flat since 1979. Contributions from manufacturing companies constituted the largest percentage until the 1980s. The top five industry contributors to education in 1988 were transportation, utilities, electrical machinery, petroleum and gas, industrial machinery, and computers.

CORPORATE GIVING TO LIBRARIES
Corporate giving to libraries in general averaged 22 percent in 1987. This figure was derived from a survey of 231 libraries including public, state, and academic institutions. Very little data is available on the types of projects supported. A 1990 survey of 16 academic research libraries revealed that corporate contributions averaged only 7 percent of total gifts, with an average contribution of just over $50,000 in the latest fiscal year. (Refer to Appendix A.)

The largest gift category was for capital support, followed by operating support; the smallest category was for endowment. The largest type of gift was outright cash, followed by equipment and other in-kind gifts. Matching gifts continue to be an important source of support.

UNIVERSITY PRIORITIES

In developing a corporate relations program, the academic research library must be especially sensitive to the university's overall priorities, including unrestricted giving and targeted campaigns. The library will benefit from an aggressive internal advocacy strategy, with strong leadership from the library director, to ensure participation in any university-wide comprehensive campaign. The key theme should be the "expansion of the pie": by including the library in major university development efforts, the institution should be able to enhance its overall fundraising results. The library development office must be particularly vigilant about the designation of matching gifts. If the donor's company restricts matching contributions to the university's unrestricted fund, the library development office may wish to urge the donor to make a special request to the company on behalf of the library.

The most successful library development programs interface actively with the corporate relations office of the university's central development department. This not only maximizes prospect research, but also ensures efficient prospect clearance. The presence of a renowned business school may pose a significant challenge in corporate prospect clearance. Fostering positive relations between the central development department and the library's administration should streamline this process.

EXTERNAL ADVOCACY

External advocacy is another critical element in a successful corporate relations program for the library. The importance of high level corporate volunteer leadership cannot be overlooked. Library development staff are charged with enabling key volunteers or trustees to "buy into" the concept of the library as the center/heart of the university. Recognize that not all volunteers are diehard bibliophiles. Create opportunities for volunteers to become enthusiastically involved in designated library projects. Become well informed about the interests of particular corporations and then match these interests with library priorities.

There is a wide variety of projects that may attract corporate support. Whenever feasible the library should emphasize the option of the multiyear pledge, which may offer a more realistic giving plan for corporations. Apart from direct contributions, there are a number of in-kind opportunities (especially computer hardware and other equipment) to support the library's technological capability. In-kind services, such as pro bono services for publications, should also be pursued. Events sponsorship offers corporations high visibility and gives the library an opportunity to expand its donor base. Endowed book funds to honor retiring executives are a dignified and underused tribute. Book endowment reinforces to corporate supporters the importance of acquisitions to the library's growth.

A corporation will typically review a number of questions when considering a proposal:

1. Will the gift enhance the corporation's image?
2. Will the donor provide reciprocal service?
3. How many employees live near the institution?

These and other elements are covered thoroughly in *Corporate Giving: Policy and Practice* by Frank Koch. The library might consider proposals to fund public service activities, which offer strong appeal to the corporation in enhancing "its long-range success and survival."

RECOGNITION

The library development office must be particularly sensitive to the need for creative recognition of corporate contributions. While the standard bronze plaque can be quite appropriate for bricks-and-mortar gifts, some corporate contributors may prefer the subtlety of a beautifully designed bookplate. The nonbibliophile may respond enthusiastically to name recognition on a computer screen for a gift of software.

SERVICES TO CORPORATIONS

Many libraries offer corporate borrowing privileges for a fee. Establishing a fee-based information service that can respond comprehensively to the needs of the business community may also, with proper planning, allow library staff to devote more time to serving the needs of their primary constituency: faculty and students. Apart from the obvious advantage of generating additional revenues for the library, a fee-based information service can lead to enhanced development opportunities within the corporate sector. Some academic institutions have tied the library's fee-based information service to an industrial liaison program, which can broaden overall development possibilities for the institution.

STEWARDSHIP

Proper stewardship is critical to the success of the library's corporate relations program. Timely and responsible compliance with the corporation's stated reporting guidelines will ensure positive long-term benefits. The institution's central development department can provide guidance on this important process.

ESTABLISHING A PROGRAM

A successful corporate relations program at an academic research library requires the proper infrastructure, both external and internal. The external infrastructure requires a highly visible volunteer presence. The library friends board or advisory board should seek representatives from key business and civic leaders of the community. Such a strategy usually begins with a core group of highly motivated volunteers or trustees who share a common interest in the library's mission. With strong volunteer leadership, this group will expand and become more focused on fundraising. As with any effective volunteer board, there will be a mix of retired and working professionals. The key to building a corporate presence for the library is to shape the volunteer board with solid representation from many industries. The library must recognize that geography will influence a corporation's funding preferences. A creative twist to geographic restrictions from the corporate headquarters is to determine the percentage of alumni employed by the corporation and to highlight the number of alumni/employees working in the geographic area of the academic institution.

INTERNAL INFRASTRUCTURE

The external infrastructure will only be effective if the internal infrastructure is firmly in place. The library director must be a visionary leader with a clear sense of the library's mission and goals. This leadership must be supported by the library's administration through clarification of priorities. The library development office must interface with the corporate relations office to select projects of potential interest to prospective corporate donors. The library's priorities must be synchronized with overall priorities of the institution. The central development department can also assist with reviews of recognition options.

CORPORATE GIVING PROGRAMS

There are several categories of corporate giving programs. Corporations without a foundation generally operate through a *direct giving program*. Gifts are often in-kind. Aggressive and persistent contacts through alumni and volunteers are especially important. Prospect research should focus on companies with products attractive to libraries (e.g., publishing, recording, and computer equipment). Generally, solicitation is informal with minimal written guidelines.

Corporations with a *contributions committee* are usually larger and have more formal and elaborate guidelines. Alumni or volunteer connections with corporate officers and directors are essential.

Matching gift programs are an ongoing opportunity for support. Be very clear about the company's policy regarding designations, and closely monitor internal recordkeeping to assure proper credit to the library's account.

Corporate *foundations* are the most formal kind of corporate giving programs, usually with elaborate guidelines. In applying for support, the library will certainly rely on guidance and assistance from the corporate relations office of the central development department. Depending on their leadership, corporate foundations tend to shift their priorities to changing areas of interest.

SUMMARY

Since the academic research library shares a natural affinity for information distribution with corporations, the library will clearly benefit from establishing an effective corporate relations component within the overall library development program. The library will need to be increasingly sensitive to the major restructuring facing many industries in Corporate America today. With the evolution of an interdependent global economy, the library would do well to explore the possibilities of corporate support from non-U.S. companies. High-level volunteer connections are central to the success of any program. Internal support from the library's administration and from the central development department are also vital elements in the process. The astute library development officer will focus on corporations' increasing sense of social responsibility. In the words of Clifton Garvin, Exxon Corporation: "To *stay* in business, we have to make a profit. To *succeed* in business, we have to share some of that profit, beyond the dividends and taxes we pay, for the public good."

APPENDIX A

SURVEY OF CORPORATE GIVING

During 1990, Northwestern University Library's Development Office conducted a survey of 30 academic research libraries that are members of DORAL (Development Officers of Research Academic Libraries): 17 public institutions and 13 private institutions. The following is a summary of the findings of that survey.

1. While responses were received from all 30 libraries, 14 reported that less than 1 percent of their total gifts were derived from corporate support.
2. Data from the other 16 libraries revealed the following:
   —The mean dollar amount of corporate giving for the latest fiscal year was $51,800.
   —The range of corporate giving for the latest fiscal year included a high of $137,400 and a low of $2,500.
   —Respondents were asked to indicate corporate giving as a percentage of total giving to the library in the latest fiscal year; the mean was 7.1 percent, with 25 percent as the high and 1 percent as the low.
3. Categories of corporate giving (in order of frequency): capital support, operating support, endowment.
4. Type of support (in order of frequency): cash, equipment, in-kind service/gift, events sponsorship.
5. Recognition/benefits (in order of frequency): plaque, library services, bookplate, computer screen.

APPENDIX B

RESOURCES

1. *Taft Corporate Giving*: an annual study of more than 550 profiles of corporations giving over $250,000 (direct giving or through foundation); information on headquarters, operations, officers/directors—with education information; indexes of giving interests (note: libraries are included under art and humanities).
2. *Corporate 1000*: A quarterly publication of the Monitor Publishing Company; 1,000 leading U.S. companies; officers/titles/addresses; type of giving.
3. *Directory of International Corporate Giving in America*: A Taft publication.
4. *Directory of American Research and Technology*: Published by R.R. Bowker's Database Publishers Group. The directory details corporate giving through R&D of corporations (i.e., operating budget vs. foundation giving).
5. *National Directory of Corporate Giving*: Published by the Foundation Center.
6. *Corporate Foundation Profiles*: Published by the Foundation Center.
7. *Who Knows Who? Networking through Corporate Boards*: An annual publication by Jeanette Glynn.
8. *Standard & Poor's*: Company reports.
9. *Corporate Giving Watch*: A monthly pamphlet published by the Foundation Center.
10. Company reports: Annual reports, 10K's.
11. In-house research from central development office of the academic institution.

ENDNOTES

1. Roger H. Parent, ed. *The ALA Yearbook of Library and Information Services '88* (Precision Typographers, Beverly Shores, Indiana, 1988), II: 189.
2. Anne Klepper, "What Lean and Mean Really Means," *Across the Board*, 24, No. 1 (January 1987): 18-19.
3. Mary Mauksch, *Corporate Voluntary Contributions in Europe* (New York: The Conference Board, Inc., 1982): 1.3
4. Maureen Nevin Duffy, *Survey of Corporate Contributions*, 1990 Ed. (New York: The Conference Board, 1990): 2-3.
5. Barbara F. Fischler, "Library Fund-Raising in the United States: A Preliminary Report," *Library Administration & Management*, (January 1987): 33.
6. Frank Koch, *Corporate Giving: Policy and Practice* (New York: The Presidents Association, 1987): 23.
7. James F. Harris and Anne Klepper, *Corporate Philanthropic Public Service Activities* (New York: The Conference Board, Inc., 1976): 8.
8. Nick Kotz, "Corporate Philanthropy: The Issues Today," *Corporate Philanthropy—Philosophy Management Trends Future Background* (Washington, D.C.: Council on Foundations, 1982): 16.

6 THE LIBRARY CAMPAIGN

by Linda J. Safran

INTRODUCTION

You have probably heard many times, "The library is the heart of your university!" Although we all believe this, the library often has a difficult time attracting the attention and funding it needs. Alumni have been carefully cultivated over the years to feel a strong allegiance to the university itself, to their department, and even to the athletic teams. But, what kind of allegiance do they have to their library?

Some libraries have a very long history of receiving strong support. It begins when the president of the university extols the library's resources to incoming freshmen and suggests that both as students and especially later as alumni, they appreciate and support the library.

I learned a great deal about library fundraising one afternoon touring a new multimillion dollar library addition at a prominent university with its director. The addition was a beautiful structure in perfect architectural harmony with the existing building. It housed an exceedingly impressive collection. But, more than the bricks and mortar and books, I was struck by the many ways this library focused on people—the people it serves now and those who helped make their university and its library what it is today. This focus was exhibited in the congenial and comfortable atmosphere, in the attractive display of student collections and alumni memorabilia, and in a memorial of names in the light well. I truly felt the heart of this university could be found within these walls.

I asked my host the secret of his success. He smiled slowly and said, "I'm just very nice to everyone the President sends over here!"

Many libraries are not blessed with this kind of support, and I suspect that there is much more to his development plan than simply "being nice." But the lesson for me that fall afternoon was that it is certainly possible to achieve this kind of success. So the first questions are:

- How can the library be made an important focus of an institution's fundraising efforts?
- Can a special library campaign assist in achieving that goal?

Your university is probably either already engaged in a major campaign or is planning one now. It is essential that the library have a prominent place in this comprehensive plan. Even if yours will be a distinct library drive run independently of the campus-wide campaign, you will always be campaigning within the broader institutional context. Therefore, to be successful you will need the blessing and support of your president and deans. Tailoring your efforts to the institutional campaign can also, to borrow loosely from Hamlet, be just the thing to "catch the conscience" of all those who talk of the library as your institutions's heart.

The following is intended to guide you through some of the questions you may have as you consider launching a campaign. If you decide to go forward, the key to your success will be good leadership, planning, and involvement within the library; good communication with and support from your central development office and the divisions; good financial and volunteer support from your major donors and friends groups; and a creative, optimistic approach to library development. A lot of energy and a good sense of humor will help, too!

WHAT? WHY? WHEN?

A library campaign is a well-defined, well-organized fundraising effort to generate a specific amount of money for specific purposes over a finite period of time. Ask yourself, "For what purposes do I need to raise funds?"

Some of these might be:

- Building and renovations
- Collection development and endowment
- Cataloging, retrospective conversions
- Special collections
- Collection development
- Computerization and equipment
- Preservation
- General endowment
- General library use (unrestricted)

Once you've decided to proceed, other questions you might consider include:

- What will be the time span for the campaign?

- What other campus fundraising will be going on at the same time?
- What external fundraising efforts might impact on the campaign?
- What are the potential internal and external obstacles?
- What factors predict success for the campaign?

FUNDING SOURCES

It is essential to identify potential funding sources. Next, ask yourself:

- Have I identified and cultivated individuals to be solicited for lead gifts?
- Are there institutional prospects that would donate to the library if asked?
- Can I make a convincing argument why each should become a library or joint donor?
- Do projected gifts from these groups total 50 percent of the goal?
- Does the library have a strong friends group with a track record of giving annually in increasing amounts?
- Could the friends be counted on to provide additional campaign support?

THE CAMPAIGN WITHIN THE CAMPAIGN

The Library Director and the Director of Library Development must have a keen understanding of the way in which fundraising priorities and decisions are made at the institution. Success will depend on support from the president, provost, deans, and faculty as well as the other development officers. It is essential to estimate how a campaign for the library fits into other current or future plans before you present the campaign plan to your central development group. To help you prepare your proposal, here are some more questions to consider:

- To whom should the concept of a library campaign be presented?
- Who should make the presentation?
- How should it be presented?
- When should it be presented?
- Do I have a lead donor lined up?
- What specific agreements can you secure?
- Who can be solicited?

- For how long can prospects be solicited?
- How will arbitration between divisions be handled?
- Who will be responsible for solicitation visits, letters, phone calls?
- Should a formal feasibility study of the potential campaign be done? Who will pay for it?
- Will I need a separate campaign budget? Where will these funds come from?

SOLICITING GIFTS

Once you have decided to launch a campaign, it will be time to formally announce the preliminary plans to your staff. A campaign will mean a great deal of the director's time and some of the library's resources in order to increase these resources for the future.

Once the preliminary plan is approved by your institution, it should be articulated by the librarian and each department should be asked to consider how the campaign goals affect their departments and how they can help meet these goals. It is also the library director's responsibility to address the expectations of the staff, and to encourage and support their enthusiasm. You should identify specific ways staff can assist as volunteers. For example, research will be needed for major prospects: individual, corporate, and foundation. You may need extra help for special events and for tours. Staff may also wonder if they will be asked to donate to the campaign. Since solicitation of your staff is a highly sensitive topic, you will want to give this careful attention. If you decide there will be a staff solicitation, this would be the time to explain what will happen and to announce participation rate goals. The library director should also include a campaign status report in whatever internal reports that are announced or circulated to staff during the campaign. You are sure to find many talented, creative staff members who will be a great help to the library during the campaign.

THE CAMPAIGN COMMITTEE

The library director and director of development, with the assistance of the central development office, should identify who will participate in the first committee meetings and tentatively who will participate in succeeding meetings. Important questions to answer are:

- What is the mission of the Campaign Committee?
- Will members be asked to help plan and implement the campaign goals? solicit gifts? donate? volunteer their time?
- Who should be chairperson?
- How many people should be on the committee?
- Who should serve on the committee?
- How will the committee interface with existing library volunteer groups such as the friends and with other groups such as the trustees?
- How often will the committee meet?
- Will there be a need for subcommittees?
- Who will staff the committee?

A FEW QUESTIONS ABOUT RESOURCES

- What current resources will be reallocated for the campaign? The Library Director's time? Equipment? Publications (brochures, newsletter, etc.)? Staff?
- What new budget allocations will be needed for staff? A full- or part-time Director of Development? Support staff? A research assistant?
- Will gift processing software and training be needed?
- Will there be any special events associated with the campaign?

CAMPAIGN DOCUMENTS

The Development Officer should create a campaign statement that states its goals clearly. The statement should include a succinct mission statement, which will be used throughout the campaign.

The director of development should create a sample proposal to be tailored for each major prospect. A simple, attractive campaign brochure also can be helpful in explaining what the campaign is for, why funds are needed now, what kinds of gifts may be made, and whom to call for more information.

SPECIAL EVENTS

A successful special event can be a great help to your fundraising efforts. The event itself is a preliminary fundraising goal and is a good opportunity to acknowledge your first big donors. It will take the time and effort of many people, so now is the time to anticipate what your needs may be.

- What kind of event will launch the campaign?
- Who will announce the campaign?
- On what occasion will it be announced?
- In what ways will it be announced?
- How will different prospect groups be informed—major library donors, other library donors, major institutional donors, other university donors, current and former library staff, students, parents, alumni, current and former faculty?
- What intermediate goals will be used for special events?
- What concluding event might be appropriate?
- Do I have the capacity to organize major special events or will I need assistance?

SOLICITING GIFTS

A good structure for the campaign gives a focus to your fundraising plan that should be helpful to you and your volunteer solicitors. The development director should create a good tracking system for the top donors and prospects that includes name, city, class, year, library gifts, total gifts, goal in dollars, staff, and action items. This list will need to be reviewed and revised continuously during the campaign and will serve as your main tracking document.

With the aid of this structure, you can ask yourself:

- Who will participate in meetings to rate prospects?
- How often will these sessions take place?
- Do the volunteers need training, including some basic information about planned giving? Will they solicit in teams?

In completing the "action items" section, each prospect should be rated according to his or her ability and readiness to give. You should also identify what cultivation needs to occur before the prospect is asked to contribute and who should make the final solicitation.

It will be important to methodically "work your list." Many times the hardest part of the development officer's job is to follow-up regularly (and tactfully) to make sure all the "action items" assigned are handled as promised. Remember to meet regularly with solicitors to review their progress and revise your goals and list accordingly.

WAS YOUR CAMPAIGN A SUCCESS?

Was it worth it? Basically, your answer is probably "Yes!" Here is yet another set of questions to help you arrive at a more specific answer:

- Did we meet our dollar goal?
- Was there an increase in the number of donors overall?
- Was there an increase in the number of alumni donors?
- Was there an increase in the average gift?
- Were more people solicited than before?

There are other things which are difficult to measure precisely, but you should try to evaluate your campaign in these areas as well:

- Was there a significant increase in awareness of library needs?
- Did the quality of our publications improve during the campaign?
- Did we increase our capacity to handle special events?
- Have stewardship, donor recognition, and cultivation strategies improved as a result of the campaign?
- Are more of the library staff now actively involved in fundraising functions?
- Are the students more aware of the importance of their library? (If so, some fundraiser will certainly thank you 50 years from now!)
- Does the library better meet the needs of the faculty as a result of the campaign?

• Has there been increased cooperation among development efforts as a result of the campaign?

In conclusion, a campaign can be an excellent way to raise funds for the library. Although the results will be measured primarily in dollars raised and goals achieved, a successful campaign will also help pave the way for other successful campaigns. Best wishes in all your efforts!

7 PLANNED GIVING

by Alison Wheeler Lahnston

Until recently, planned giving was considered a catchall branch of development that dealt with specialized gifts of securities, deferred gifts such as trusts and annuities, bequests, and gifts-in-kind. In effect, such a department primarily handled difficult gifts with tax implications, frequently from older donors, which typically did not result in current unrestricted money for the recipient. With the growing complexity of the tax laws and the increasing sophistication of donors, however, virtually every major gift today has tax implications and is carefully structured to assist the donor with his or her taxes, estate planning, and, often, to provide income to the donor as well as to the institution.

Planned giving now creatively matches the needs of the donor to those of the institution using tax expertise and a wide variety of giving options. Formerly product-oriented, planned giving is now proactive and service-oriented. Fundraisers who once described themselves as officers for deferred giving have, for the most part, come to call themselves officers of planned giving. To emphasize the service orientation of their work, a number of schools (including Harvard and Brown universities) now have offices of gift planning.

BENEFITS TO DONORS

By whatever name, planned giving is vital to the ongoing health of the research library, both as a way to encourage donors to increase the size of their current gifts and to ensure a continuing stream of endowment income in the future. Planned giving strategies enable the donor to:

1. Increase the size of the current gift by giving away assets no longer wanted or needed, such as securities or real estate.
2. Create or add to the collections through in-kind gifts of books, manuscripts, and so forth.
3. Endow the maintenance of the donor's papers or collections already given through bequests.
4. Endow current gifts by setting up bequests with endowment provisions for book funds, preservation funds, or,

best of all, for unrestricted money to be used at the discretion of the librarian.

ORIGINS OF PLANNED GIVING

Planned giving as a means of creating support for the library is a technique that has its roots in the last century. Bequests and annuities were the first vehicles. The Treasurer's Report of Harvard University of 1829, for example, notes two bequests and the use of them to create an endowment: "The Legacies of Thomas Hollis and Samuel Shapleigh, being both for the Library, without any limitation or restriction, might be conveniently carried to one account, to be styled the Library Fund."[1] The library then was as central to the institution's mission as it is now. The "Estimate of the Expenses of a Student at Harvard College for one year, as reduced by the Corporation after August 31, 1828," was $206. The first and largest charge, for $90, was "for instruction, use of Library, Lecture Rooms, Steward's Department, Rent, and Care of Rooms," and the second charge of $20 was for "class books delivered from the Library."

Planned giving is now a vital component of any development plan. Bequests are a key element of a charity's balanced budget, and a well-run planned giving office may be responsible for 20 to 30 percent of total annual giving. For example, figures from the Ivy-MIT-Stanford Conference for fiscal year 1989 show planned giving as a range of total giving from 16 to 31 percent.[2] Recent university campaigns have raised as much as 34 percent of their total in planned gifts.[3]

THE OFFICER'S ROLE

The constant need for new and greater sources of support has made modern fundraising an increasingly complex and sophisticated task. Today, the typical work week of a planned giving officer for the library might include helping a donor and his attorney word a bequest to endow a book fund for the purchase of Portuguese and Brazilian materials; arranging a meeting with administrators to go over terms for the creation of an endowed library position, to be funded with a combination of an outright gift of securities, proceeds from the sale of a piece of real estate, and a bequest provision; helping a widow to establish a book fund in memory of her husband, funding the eventual endowment through a charitable gift annuity; meeting a member of the library visiting committee to review a list of names for possible new library prospects; and ensuring that a past donor receives a report of the purchases from her endowed funds that have added to the collection she has already given the library.

While few, if any, research libraries have a full-time planned giving officer, virtually all of them have the services of a planned giving or gift planning office. Whatever assistance available, however, the steps you need to take to identify, cultivate, solicit, and steward planned giving prospects are much the same as those you will take to identify major gift prospects. It is always heartening when donors respond to a planned giving mailing or walk in the door asking to make a planned gift—but, realistically, you will have to identify most of the new prospects yourself.

IDENTIFICATION OF PROSPECTS

The first step toward identifying prospects for planned giving is to look at current donor lists. Individuals who have already made several smaller gifts are ideal candidates to move up to a higher giving level. These people have been described elsewhere in this book.

When you have exhausted your current donor base, enlarge your search and begin to identify new prospects. Libraries appeal to almost everyone who went to college; they are central to the mission of any educational institution. As Henry Rosovsky, former dean of the Faculty of Arts and Sciences at Harvard University, points out, libraries are to humanists and social scientists what laboratories are to physical scientists—the center of their research and learning. Almost everyone has positive feelings about libraries, and examples of the skyrocketing costs of books, periodicals, space, and cataloging are some of the easiest ways to get people to understand why education is so expensive today and to respond by giving. To increase your donor pool, consider ways to qualify prospects from the following groups—alumni, major givers, users of all kinds, and faculty.

CULTIVATION OF PROSPECTS

Cultivation techniques have been described in other chapters and are applicable here as well, but a few techniques are particularly useful for planned giving prospects.

VISITS AND CALLS

With older planned giving prospects, a preliminary letter will prepare someone who may be hard-of-hearing to expect your phone call and will help pave the way for a visit. Every visit should also, of course, be followed by a thank-you letter. The letter may contain a response to a question you could not answer during the visit or even a proposal for a planned gift, but its chief purpose is to pave the way for further visits by you or someone else at your institution. The management of these visits, phone calls, and letters should be the daily concern of every planned giving fundraiser.

MAILING

Less effective than visits but certainly necessary, mailings will reach even those planned giving prospects you have not been able to identify, cultivate them, and bring them to the point where they identify themselves. Then you can make personal contact. A sampling of mailings might include:

- Planned giving brochures with a cover letter. Virtually all universities send out planned giving materials to anniversary classes. Make sure that these brochures include the library or book funds as possible ways to designate a planned gift.
- All planned giving ads appearing in your alumni or institutional magazine or even your athletic programs should include a mention of the library or book funds as a worthy recipient of a gift.
- Library-specific mailings are effective in reaching prospects, especially past donors, and emphasize the important role gifts play in the library's budget. If your library has a newsletter, make sure recent gifts of collections, bequests, and other planned gifts are given prominence. Include photographs of the donors in every possible case.

• Annual reports. Most donors enjoy seeing their gifts recognized in the annual report. Every library can profit from an annual list of donors. By highlighting the planned giving, their importance is emphasized. The Annual Report of the Harvard University Library, for example, not only lists all members of the visiting committee and all sustaining friends of the library (those giving $500 or more), but also lists major donors to the special collections and libraries, as well as those who have added to or created new endowment funds. Most important for our purposes, it highlights a list of "donors of planned gifts for library endowments" and another of "trust programs." While the function here is primarily stewardship, these lists also help arouse the curiosity and raise the sights of new prospects. Furthermore, an annual report can be a nice gift to leave behind after a visit.

CAUTION

One final caution about the timing of cultivation efforts. Experienced development officers and librarians develop a special sensitivity to approaching prospects who are undergoing significant changes in their lives such as a new job, retirement, or the death of a spouse. I had the wretched experience once of travelling six hours to visit a prospect only to find out his wife had died three days before, he had been too upset to think to cancel our visit, and he was about to leave for the funeral. An apology on my part, immediate departure, and a condolence letter were certainly in order. It is almost equally tactless to approach a distinguished faculty member for his papers the moment his retirement is announced in the school bulletin. As Helen Samuels, institute archivist of the Massachusetts Institute of Technology, has noted,

Societal attitudes and personal concerns about retirement place a great psychological weight on faculty members approaching their departure. Fears that their productive years are at an end can therefore be reinforced by the archivist who asks for their manuscript collection at this moment. If their work is to continue they still need their papers. Archivists should work with faculty and other donors earlier in their career so that the solicitation of their collection becomes a compliment about their productive career, and not a confirmation that they are washed up.

WAYS TO GIVE

The most popular planned giving options are life income gifts, charitable lead trusts, bequests and gifts of securities, tangible personal property, and real estate. Each option is described briefly in the following sections.

LIFE INCOME GIFTS

Annuities, pooled income funds, and trusts account for the vast majority of planned gifts. Each provides that the donor make a gift and in return the donor or another beneficiary receives income from the trust or other fund over his or her lifetime. Ultimately, upon the death of the donor, the library receives the interest as well as the capital from the gift. The most popular life income gifts are:

Charitable Gift Annuities: A gift annuity is a contract between the donor and the library. The donor makes a gift to the library and receives:

- Guaranteed fixed payments for life, a portion of which are nontaxable
- A charitable income tax deduction for a portion of the gift amount and
- The satisfaction of contributing to support of the library

Because the payment rate on an annuity is based on the amount of the annuity and the age of the beneficiary(ies) at the time the gift is made, gift annuities are especially appropriate for donors age 55 and older. The rates are established by the Nationwide Committee on Charitable Gift Annuities, composed of representatives from educational, religious, and charitable institutions.

Younger prospects who are in a high tax bracket now may want to consider a deferred gift annuity. Payments may be deferred for a number of years—often until retirement—but the donor receives a tax deduction immediately.

Charitable gift annuities may be funded with cash, securities, or property. Payouts may be established on an annual, semi-annual or quarterly basis. Mailing these checks is an excellent opportunity to send greetings to donors, update them on events at the library, or provide them with the latest tax tips. The language for an annuity need not be elaborate; the Committee on Gift Annuities or your institution's counsel can readily supply examples. Most institutions require a gift of at least $5,000 or $10,000 to write an annuity; a smaller figure is not cost effective for the library.

Pooled Income Funds: A pooled income fund is very similar to a mutual fund and operates in much the same way. A donor's gift is commingled with other gifts and assigned a proportionate share in the fund. The fund is usually managed by a bank or by your institution's financial managers. The current earnings of the fund— all dividends and interest—are paid to the beneficiaries, usually quarterly. The donor may name a second beneficiary. The gift provides an immediate tax deduction to the donor based on the size of the gift, the age of the beneficiaries and the historical return of the fund. Typically, only cash or securities may be contributed to a pooled income fund, but if the donor uses long-term appreciated securities to make the gift, there is the additional benefit of avoiding payment of any capital gains tax. Pooled income funds have an additional advantage over annuities: the rate of return varies and, in times of rapidly rising interest rates, can generally provide a very real hedge against inflation. On the death of the last beneficiary, the library receives the principal to be used as designated by the donor.

Pooled income funds can be established with various investment performance goals in mind—growth funds, high-yield funds, or a balance of the two. Larger institutions will frequently have several funds which offer investment objectives from which a donor may choose. In each case make sure the gift is clearly earmarked for the library.

If your institution does not now have a pooled fund consider starting one. A good tax attorney can provide the necessary documentation to set it up and get it approved. Unless you anticipate a very large fund it is more trouble than it is worth to manage the investments and complex calculations of shares and quarterly payments internally; major banks provide these services at reasonable fees.

Charitable Remainder Trusts: If your donor has specific investment objectives in mind and the gift is large enough to make separate management cost-effective, you may want to offer him or her the option of a charitable trust. A trust is a separate legal entity. The assets are managed as separate accounts either by your institution or by a trustee of the donor's choice. Typically, a minimum of $50,000 or $100,000 is required to make writing a separate trust cost-effective. A charitable remainder trust offers the advantage of providing income to the donor or another beneficiary with an immediate charitable tax deduction in the year the gift is made. Assets used to fund charitable trusts may include cash, securities, or almost any property of marketable value. Real estate that is not producing income for the donor and low yielding but highly appreciated securities are two of the most commonly used assets to fund trusts. Tax exempt securities can also be used to fund a trust, thus producing tax free income. After the death of the last beneficiary the remainder of the trust passes to the charity (hence the name).

There are two other types of charitable remainder trusts: a *charitable remainder annuity trust* provides a fixed amount of income to the beneficiary at a rate established when the trust is written; a *charitable remainder unitrust* provides an income-based fixed percentage of the assets in the trust as revalued annually. Like the pooled income fund, a unitrust can provide a hedge against inflation, and careful management that increases the value of the assets in a unitrust can often provide both increased income and a larger remainder value to the library. Because a charitable remainder annuity trust guarantees a fixed income to the beneficiary, no additions may be made to the principal. A unitrust may, however, be added to at any time and is often a favorite vehicle for annual additions by the donor.

Charitable Lead Trusts: A charitable lead trust is a mirror image of a remainder trust. Assets are set aside in a trust. The income goes to the library for a specified period of years and the assets revert after the period of years to the donor or his or her designees. If the assets are transferred to the donor's heirs, any increase in the value of the trust is free of gift and estate taxes. As a result, it may be possible to pass on to heirs a larger estate. In addition, the gift tax due in the year the trust is created is reduced by a deduction equal to the present value of the income to the library. For the library, the advantage of receiving the immediate income from the trust is readily apparent. And in spite of new tax laws, which limit to some extent the advantages of the lead trust, it remains one of a very few ways to shelter property—and any future appreciation—from the generation-skipping transfer tax and thus providing for donor's heirs. A skilled lawyer, expert in tax matters, is especially necessary for the creation of a proper charitable lead trust, but the benefits to all concerned are obvious. In Harvard's last capital campaign, three of the largest gifts were made in this form.

GIFTS OF SECURITIES

Although not strictly a planned gift, gifts of securities are frequently used to fund planned gifts. If your donor has securities that have been held long-term and have appreciated in value, he or she may be reluctant to sell them because of capital gains taxes. By giving them to your library directly or using them to fund a life-income gift, capital gains taxes are avoided. If, in addition, the securities have been low-yielding, the donor may be pleasantly surprised at how much more income he or she can now receive. The donor can typically claim a charitable gift deduction equal to the full fair-market value of the securities at the time of transfer. For a very small number of donors the gain on some gifts of long-term appreciated property may be subject to the alternative minimum tax. A good planned giving software package can easily make the calculations to see if this tax applies. If it does you may want to suggest to your donor's financial advisor that the gift be spread out over several years; your donor will thank you for those tax savings.

If the donor is an owner or a partner of a corporation you may wish to suggest a gift of securities through the corporation, entitling the corporation to a charitable deduction. Even if the stock is nonmarketable stock from a closely held corporation you can accept this gift. The closely held stock can be bought back by the corporation as long as there is no legal obligation of your charity to redeem it.

The easiest way to make a gift of securities is by electronic transfer between the donor's broker and your gift or treasurer's office. If the donor has physical possession of the certificates, instruct him or her to mail them *unsigned* to you and, in a *separate* envelope, to mail you a signed stock power for each certificate. If the gift is made in late December be sure to keep the postmarked envelope as proof of the gift's tax year.

In recent years, zero coupon bonds as gifts have become more popular with donors. These bonds do not pay interest until maturity which is often many years away and consequently are low in cost. While zero coupon bonds are legitimate gifts, they may be a problem to your institution for two reasons. First, your treasurer may have to hold them for many years in order to realize their value. This could be in conflict with your investment policy. Many policies require that every gift be sold and reinvested to reflect the institutional investment policy and portfolio mix. Second, your donor may ask to have the maturity value of the bond credited while a more realistic policy is to credit the cost of the bonds to your donor. One way around the first difficulty is to suggest to the donor that the bonds be used to fund a charitable remainder trust for his or her retirement or grandchildren. An "income only" remainder trust will provide for a payout only if there is income the donor can provide. Then when the bonds mature and produce such income, it goes to the donor for retirement purposes or to the donor's heirs in the form of income.

The crediting issue will only be resolved if you explain to your donor that you can give credit only for the actual value of the gift received—the cost of the bond to the donor.

GIFTS IN-KIND

Libraries and art museums deal with more gifts in-kind than any other areas in research universities. Papers, collections, and even portraits and other memorabilia flood in profusely. Your first decision must be, of course, what to accept. A strong gift committee including the librarian, treasurer, and development officer with a written gift policy should be created so that the development officer is buffered from personally having to decline unwanted gifts from a prospect whose largesse you would otherwise welcome.

VALUATION AND DISPOSAL

Once you have decided to accept the gift you will need to deal with questions of valuation and disposal. All gifts of tangible personal property should be accompanied by a valuation letter from a qualified appraiser and by a letter from your donor stating that the library has the right to dispose of the item in the future. Some gifts of tangible property can be sold and the proceeds used immediately. Other gifts may be used to fund life-income arrangements for the donor.

Gifts of tangible personal property must be divided into:

1. Those which are related to the exempt purpose of the library, i.e., for an educational or research purpose.
2. Those you plan to sell or lease or put to a use that is unrelated to your exempt purpose (i.e., the gift of a car which you give to the librarian for his or her private use).
3. Those that are works of the donor.

A gift to the library of a collection of papers or a rare book will receive a charitable deduction for the full fair market value, therefore, when it is given, it is reasonable for your donor to expect that it will be put to use. If, on the other hand, the donor expects you to immediately sell the major portion or all of the gift, the donor's income tax deduction must be reduced by 40 percent of the unrealized appreciation.

For example, suppose your donor gives you a rare set of first editions by Charles Dickens that was acquired in 1975 for $100,000 and is now worth $500,000. He or she knows you already have a set and plan to sell the gift. The income tax deduction would have been $500,000 if you had kept the set, but since you are selling it, the donor may deduct only $340,000 ($500,000 less 40 percent of the $400,000 long-term appreciation, or $160,000). Note that this rule applies only to the income tax deduction; the estate and gift tax deduction is still equal to the full fair market value no matter what use is made of the gift.

So far we have been talking about tangible gifts which are not created by the donor. Manuscripts, papers, and other written materials, if written by the donor or acquired by the donor from the writer as a gift, are treated as ordinary income assets by the government. In these cases, if the donor sold the property it would be treated like an ordinary asset and the income would be taxed as an ordinary asset rather than as a capital gain. Consequently, if the donor gives them to you, he or she may deduct only the cost bases of the gift. (Note that if the donor inherited the papers, however, the gift would be deductible at full fair market value.) Because this is a complex area it is useful to consult your institution's attorney if you are in any doubt as to the valuation of the gift.

GOVERNMENT REGULATIONS

The government has become very strict about reporting gifts of tangible personal property by the donor and, as a charity, you would do well to be as helpful as possible in this area. Keep on hand copies of form 8283 "Noncash Charitable Contributions" which must accompany the donor's tax forms when he or she files, and a copy of the instructions (these are readily available by calling the Internal Revenue Service). A donor must submit this form if the deduction claimed is over $500 and must obtain a written appraisal from a qualified appraiser if the total deduction he claims is $5000 for any item or group of similar items given. (This applies even if the donor divides the gift among a number of charities, and if that is the case the donor must file a separate form for each charity.) You will be required to get an official signature for Part IV of form 8283 acknowledging receipt of the gift. If the gift is sold within two years you must also file companion form 8282 with the IRS and give the donor a copy indicating the date of sale, the goods sold, and the value received for them.

One final note on tangible personal property: because the donor has the burden of proof to establish that the gift made had a related use it is important for you to give the donor a letter indicating how you plan to use the gift.

GIFTS OF REAL ESTATE

In the current depressed real estate market, gifts of land, houses and commercial property are skyrocketing. Some gifts will be outright to support the library; the donor can then receive a tax deduction for the full fair-market value of the property, subject, of course, to any alternative minimum tax restrictions that might apply. Other gifts may be used to fund life income arrangements.

You may have a prospect who is interested in ultimately leaving you his or her home. Consider asking for it now with the stipulation that the donor live in it for the remainder of his or her life and that of a second beneficiary if they wish. The donor would continue to pay the taxes, insurance, and maintenance costs. But by giving it now, the donor would receive a substantial deduction now for the gift. Should the deduction be greater than the donor can use that year, the excess, like any other charitable deduction, can be carried over for five additional years.

Dealing with gifts of real estate is a complex business. Donors of such gifts typically want or need to have them handled extremely rapidly. In setting up your planned giving program you will want to make sure you have an external team of appraisers, real estate experts and lawyers ready to assist you and your internal team (your treasurer, counsel, and president or board). Your job is to move things along briskly, keep in constant communication with all parties and maintain a positive attitude.

As a first step you should have a prepared list of questions that ask the donors to describe the property, the history of ownership, and why they want to give it away. Second, you will need a more complete disclosure list to test the donor's sincerity and alert you to any pitfalls (lead paint, asbestos, environmental dangers such as hazardous wastes, etc.). You will need to know, for example, if there are other owners or a mortgage involved, zoning restrictions, and taxes. Third, when a thorough list is completed, you will then need a letter of understanding that spells out exactly who pays for such things as taxes, maintenance, and fees. If you pay, will the donor reimburse you? The donor will need an appraisal from a qualified appraiser and you will need your own on-site examination, title search, and true market evaluation so you will have no unpleasant surprises. Finally, you will move to the execution stage with the signing of the formal documents. Keeping your attorney, your institution, and your donor fully informed can be almost a full-time job, but ultimately the gift will repay your labors.

BEQUESTS

Bequests typically form the largest share of planned gifts. In the Ivy-MIT-Stanford group, for example, $172.6 million was raised in 1990 by bequests while trusts accounted for $143.74 million. For many donors a gift through a will is the most realistic way of making a significant contribution to the library.

A will is a legal document that allows the donor to decide to whom assets are to be distributed and in what proportions or amounts. Any type of property including cash, securities, jewelry, works of art, and real estate may be left by bequest. Explain to your donor, when you discuss estate plans, that a charitable bequest may reduce or eliminate federal and state estate taxes and that a bequest can be used to support a specific project or purpose.

Be sure that the donor is not writing restrictions into the will that could prevent your institution from accepting the gift. One common mistake is to incorrectly identify the charity. Leaving a gift "to Harvard University," for example, may mean that the gift of an alumnus of Harvard College will be spent at Harvard Divinity School. If the donor wants to make a gift to the library, make sure the correct name of the institution and the library's name is clearly spelled out. Be frank with a donor; a gift with too many restrictions is not helpful.

Some of the various forms of bequests are:

- *Specific bequest:* The library receives a specific dollar amount, percentage of the estate, or specific piece of property.
- *Residuary bequest:* The library receives all or a percentage of the estate after all other bequests, debts, taxes, and other expenses are paid.
- *Trust:* A trust may be established by will that provides for the library and other beneficiaries.
- *Contingent bequest:* The library receives a part or all of the estate under specific circumstances.

By working closely with your prospects and getting to know them you can help to avert unwanted or overly restricted bequests and provide thoughtful recognition to donors who have put the library in their wills. Make sure that every appeal from the library has a check-off box that says something along the lines of, "I have made a provision for the library in my will," or "I would like more information on how to put the library in my will." Receiving these replies is often your first step towards ensuring a significant planned gift.

CREATING A PROGRAM

In creating your planned giving program you will be working your way through the steps described in this chapter, identifying your prospects, cultivating them, soliciting them by matching their needs to planned giving vehicles, and providing stewardship.

As a first step, include a box or two on the annual appeal reply card asking the donor to indicate whether the library is included in the donor's will or if the donor would like some information on planned giving. Mail out your appeals at intervals so you will be able to respond promptly to replies and not be deluged by a pile of unanswered mail. When positive replies come in, answer at once—with a visit, if at all possible, or at least a telephone call. Now your program is underway and you can enlarge it from there.

At the same time you are contacting your first prospects you will need to be setting up your program by taking the following steps.

INTERNAL STEPS

1. Get to know your institution's officers. Meet with your treasurer, gift officer, or whoever is responsible for accepting gifts of cash, securities, real estate and gifts in-kind.

2. Go over procedures for each kind of gift. Make sure you have proper forms on hand including stock powers and forms 8282 and 8283. Draft a brief description of how to give securities, how to fill out form 8283, and how to put the library in a will.

3. Create a gift committee if one doesn't already exist so you can refer to it dubious gifts you may not want to accept.

4. Purchase a service that will keep you up to date on changes in relevant tax and estate planning law. One useful service is "Taxwise Giving" by Conrad Teitel (Philanthropy Tax Institute, 13 Arcadia Road, Old Greenwich, CT 06870; (203) 637-4311), and there are others as well.

5. Consider purchasing software that can do all your calculations for tax deductions, annuity projections, and comparisons between different types of planned giving options for a donor. An excellent one I have used at several different institutions is PG Calc (PG Calc, Inc., 129 Mt. Auburn Street, Cambridge, MA 02138; (617) 497-4970), but there are a number of other such services and you will want to make a comparison.

EXTERNAL STEPS

1. If necessary, get to know a tax attorney who will be able to help you with the fine points of closing on a planned gift. The attorney

not only needs to be extremely knowledgeable about planned giving but to have the attitude and energy that will make a gift happen rather than simply dreaming up difficulties. Discuss with the attorney the pros and cons of starting your own pooled income fund and have the language drafted if you decide to go ahead. Also, have the attorney draft a simple annuity contract you can use with your donors.

2. If you will be handling gifts of real estate find a trustworthy real estate expert who can help you realistically evaluate gifts locally and can also help you locate other real estate experts across the country if you're lucky enough to be given some property out of town.

3. Develop a list of reputable appraisers you can send to a donor who wants a collection appraised and asks you for guidance.

PROFESSIONAL STEPS

1. Take at least one good planned giving seminar. CASE, The Council for the Advancement and Support of Education (Suite 400, 11 Dupont Circle, Washington, DC 10036; (202) 328-5923), offers both beginning and advanced planned giving seminars. A very fine marketing-oriented seminar is taught both at the beginning and advanced level by John Brown (John Brown, Ltd, Inc., Noone Falls, Route 202 South, Peterborough, NH 03458; (603) 924-3834). Some other excellent seminars are conducted by Jonathan Tidd (9 Beaver Brook Road, W. Simsbury, CT 06092; (203) 651-8937); Ellen Estes and Janet Hill Otto (Estes/Otto, 41 Spoke Drive, Woodbridge, CT 06525; (203) 393-3159) and Conrad Teitel (Philanthropy Tax Institute, 13 Arcadia Road, Old Greenwich, CT 06870; (203) 637-4311).

2. Join a regional planned giving group, if possible. These professional organizations provide lectures on timely topics, generally on a monthly basis, and also put you in touch with other local professionals in the field. You will find them supportive, encouraging, and helpful as you begin your own program. The National Committee on Planned Giving (IU Center on Philanthropy, 550 West North Street, Suite 304, Indianapolis, IN 46202-3162; (317) 684-8918) can provide you with the name and address of your local chapter.

3. Begin to collect relevant materials for your own library. A good text on financial planning, a tax service (such as Teitel's mentioned above) and a how-to book such as Debra Ashton's *The Complete Guide to Planned Giving,* (J.L.A. Publications, c/o Jeffrey Lant Associates, 50 Follen Street, Suite 507, Cambridge, MA 02138, (617) 547-6372) would be a good start. You will want

to add other volumes. For example, I have found the *Harvard Manual of Planned Giving* to be very helpful (the seventh edition by David Donaldson and Carolyn Osteen is in progress and may be ordered by writing to Donaldson at Ropes and Gray, One International Place, Boston, MA 02110-2624; (617) 951-7000).

ETHICAL STEPS

Finally, consider seriously the ethics of the work you are beginning. Asking for money, being privy to an individual's most personal affairs, and representing an educational institution are serious matters. There is a tendency in planned giving to become very close to your donors and it is important to be very clear about the institution's needs, the donor's needs, and your needs. Remember, you always represent the institution and your donor should never be allowed to lose sight of that fact. In August 1990, the Canaras Group, a member council of the National Committee on Planned Giving, developed a set of sensible and useful guidelines, which are reproduced here.[4]

THE CANARAS CODE
A Code for Gift Planners (i.e., all individuals and organizations engaged in soliciting, planning, rendering advice with respect to, accepting or administering charitable gifts.)

The solicitation, planning and administration of a charitable gift is a complex process involving philanthropic, personal, tax and financial considerations.

This Code is intended to assure that the process is conducted in a professional and ethical manner that achieves a fair and proper balance between the personal interests of the donor and the purposes of the charitable institution. We recommend its adoption and observance by all Gift Planners.

1. In any solicitation or planning of a charitable gift, the Gift Planner shall give primary emphasis to the philanthropic nature of the gift; tax considerations should *not* be the primary focus of the gift. Any investment considerations

should reflect the fact that the gift is being invested, at least in part, for and on behalf of the charity.

2. The Gift Planner shall explain all aspects of a proposed charitable gift fully, fairly and accurately to the donor during the gift planning process. This explanation should include:

- the charity's proposed use of the gift;
- all fees and costs of planning and management;
- valuation issues and procedures;
- tax consequences and reporting requirements;
- alternative arrangement for making the gift;
- financial and family implications; and
- any other information which is relevant to the donor's decision to make the gift.

3. A Gift Planner shall not act or purport to act as a representative of any charity without the express(ed?) knowledge and approval of the charity and shall not, while in the employ of a charity, act or purport to act as a representative of the donor.

4. A Gift Planner acting on behalf of the charity shall encourage the donor to discuss the proposed gift with a competent lawyer or accountant of the donor's choice; a Gift Planner acting on behalf of the donor shall, where appropriate, encourage the donor to discuss the proposed gift with the charity to whom the gift is to be made.

5. Fees charged by Gift Planners shall be reasonable in relation to the services provided and shall be charged to the person to whom, or on behalf of whom, the services are provided. A Gift Planner shall not solicit, and a charity shall not pay, any fee, directly or indirectly, for the right to receive a gift.

ENDNOTES

1. Harvard University, The Treasurer's Report 1929, page 63.
2. FY '90 Ivy League—Stanford MIT Conference Data.
3. Vince Stehle, "Which Gifts Should Count in Capital Campaigns," *The Chronicle of Philanthropy,* November 13, 1990: 6.
4. Reprinted by permission of David Donaldson, Ropes and Gray, Boston, MA.

8 PUBLIC RELATIONS

by William R. Mott

Recently I was introduced to a fellow library worker as the library fundraiser. "Oh," my new friend said, "you are responsible for public relations." I laughed and agreed, "Yes, I guess I am." Her observation struck me as curious, but I did not give it much thought. Later I began to reflect on her comment and it occurred to me that she was right on target in terms of the fundraising function in academic libraries. It is indeed difficult to separate public relations and fundraising.

There is ample literature that thoroughly discusses the general topic of public relations: here discussion will be limited to the function of public relations in an academic library setting, and specifically as it bears on fundraising. Public relations is an integral component of a successful fundraising effort. It is virtually impossible to have one without the other. Public relations exists to support the university and the library, and the chances of achieving fundraising objectives are enhanced if the university has made public relations a priority in developing support for its programs.

Public relations can be described as a process of communication between the institution and the community for the purpose of increasing awareness, support, and understanding of institutional needs and priorities. This definition applies to libraries within the context of the university. In the past few years, public relations has been the subject of much interest and concern to universities all over the country. Declines in enrollment, decreasing budgets, and a widespread belief that the educational system is failing have led universities to take another look at their public relations efforts.[1] Public relations, often referred to as institutional relations in higher education, has become more aggressive in promoting its programs and activities.

While public relations in academic libraries is not an altogether new concept, it predates the idea of public relations as a component of library fundraising. Twenty years ago very few academic libraries could claim to have a clearly identified public relations program.[2] Recent events have inspired creation of some public relations programs. Others have surfaced in an effort to provide additional support for fundraising activities.

MANAGING THE EFFORT

WHERE TO START
Often the biggest obstacle to getting started is deciding what to do first. Once you have determined that fundraising along with public relations is a university and library priority, it is important to develop a comprehensive plan incorporating all aspects of what you hope to accomplish. Your effectiveness will be determined by how well-developed your plan is. Above all, your plan should support and reinforce the mission of the university and the library.

PROGRAM PLANS
There are several factors in developing a public relations plan for academic library fundraising. These factors include establishing clear goals and objectives, setting up appropriate administrative structures, addressing staffing needs, and maintaining a close working relationship both with the library and the development and institutional relations office. The setting of clearly defined and agreed upon goals and objectives is a fundamental part of establishing a successful public relations program.

An effective way to begin is to look at the events, activities, and programs that will be taking place during the year and then establish monthly and quarterly goals for public relations activities necessary to support these programs. Goals and objectives should be as specific as possible so that they are clearly measurable. For example, if you know that you want to promote the Friends of the Library annual program, then you set public relations objectives far enough ahead to allow time to make preparations. This kind of major library event should be featured in newsletters, campus and student newspapers, local and area newspapers, and on radio and television. Therefore, if this event takes place in November, then your objective should read "I will have developed and implemented a plan to promote the Friends of the Library annual program by October 1." In this way you are assured of time to properly prepare for and promote the event.

STAFFING
Staffing plays a key role in the effectiveness of your library public relations effort. Many major academic research libraries have development officers. Some have responsibility for public relations, others do not. While the immediate staff may be small, access to the development/institutional relations staff can provide the

necessary support to accomplish your communications goals. It is fundamental to understand that you do not operate in a vacuum but with a team of professionals all of whom, like you, are supporting and promoting various parts of the university, and, thereby, the university as a whole.

Often the questions are raised about the skills necessary to be successful in public relations and development. Communication skills are fundamental, both written and spoken. The ability to write proposals, newsletters, brochures, acknowledgments, and much more is essential. Spoken communication is also a must. Many times the development/public relations officer is called upon to make presentations, particularly when calling on corporations, foundations, and individual donors. The ability to clearly articulate your message will have much to do with whether or not you are successful.

Necessary skills include a high energy level coupled with a flexible nature and the ability to deal effectively with frustration. Development and public relations calls for long hours of work. Special events and activities are often held at night and on weekends. The ability to withstand the pressure of deadlines and to remain calm as you juggle several projects at once will enable you to be effective.

Above all, you must possess a complete commitment to and belief in what you are doing. Nothing will more completely convince others of your dedication than your belief that what you are doing supports the work of the institution in important ways. You will find it easy to "sell your library" to others if you enthusiastically believe in what you are doing.

The professionalism with which you do your job is also important. The desire to grow and learn new skills and techniques enhances your performance. Affiliation with professional organizations is perhaps the best way to keep abreast of developments in your field. Take full advantage of institutional affiliations with such organizations as the American Library Association (ALA), the Council for the Advancement and Support of Education (CASE), the National Society for Fund Raising Executives (NSFRE), the American College Public Relations Association (ACPRA), and possibly others.[3] These organizations publish magazines, conduct seminars and workshops, and provide other services that will help you do your job effectively.

The organizational aspects include your reporting relationship with the library administration and university development/university relations office. As stated above, this requires being a "team player." The library must work closely and in cooperation with the university to ensure that one is supporting the other. Public relations on a university-wide basis has at its core the goal of enhancing, supporting, and encouraging the image of the institution so that its important publics—groups and individuals—understand and support it.[4] The library, as a central component of the institution can benefit from public relations programs already in place.

PROMOTIONAL IDEAS

Certain techniques can focus appropriate attention on the academic library. First, review the different media you have that could function in support of your intended goal. In the area of print media the possibilities include newsletters, alumni publications, brochures, and newspapers. Nonprint of course includes radio and television. What it is that you are trying to promote will determine which media mix will garner the best result. For example, is your audience within the university or are you attempting to communicate with the larger community? Do you seek national coverage, or is local coverage what you are after?

SELECTING PUBLICITY ACTIVITIES

What activities do you want to publicize that will demonstrate the library's call to service, secure large amounts of good will, and have a direct impact on fundraising efforts.[5] First, look to your own collections, those unique holdings that distinguish your research collections from others. What do you have that might say to friends and donors, "this is our signature collection?" Events that focus attention on what makes you special are the best kind. Give careful thought to the people you want involved. For example, the presence of a member of the university board of trustees sends the signal that this event is significant and warrants the interest of the entire university community. Recently at Emory University, Mr. Robert Goizueta, chairman of the board of Coca-Cola Company and an Emory trustee, spoke at the opening of the library's Robert Woodruff Centennial Exhibition. His appearance had impact: it conveyed to the public that the library can attract important people to its events. That recognition can generate support for many programs and attract other influential people to future events.

ANNIVERSARIES

Celebrating and recognizing anniversaries is another way to attract attention to the university library. The Johns Hopkins University Library recently celebrated its 25th anniversary. Over 1,400 people turned out for this occasion. Noted author Tom Wolfe was awarded an honorary doctorate and gave a rousing speech followed by a reception. The event was featured in the libraries' newsletter (see Figure 8-1). The tremendous amount of publicity generated will have long-lasting implications and while the work involved in the planning and execution may be burdensome, the results will be felt for long after the event is over. Such an investment of time and effort pays handsome dividends in achievement of your public relations objectives.

FRIENDS PROGRAMS

Be alert to every opportunity to call attention to the library. Friends of the Library organizations often sponsor several programs throughout the year. At Vanderbilt University, a nationally known author is asked to speak at an annual dinner each fall (Figure 8-2). Always a popular event, this lays the foundation for various types of support, including financial contributions, gifts of collections, and gifts of time. Planning and executing a book sale is another opportunity for people to volunteer their time to the library. Volunteer participation in your program is essential because it creates an atmosphere of partnership.

Each event builds on the next. These occasions should not be viewed as standing alone, separate from each other. Each should be part of your overall strategy to involve as many people as possible and thereby secure more support for your library. A variety of activities will reach the largest number of friends. Developing and educating a base of supporters who can be called upon to help the library realize its financial and collection goals should be at the heart of your public relations program.

FIGURE 8-1 Newsletter Features 25th Anniversary Celebration

Ex Líbrís

New Series, Vol. XII, No. 3, Spring 1990

The Johns Hopkins University Libraries

XXV: Eisenhower Library Celebrates Its Twenty-fifth Anniversary

Bob Stockfield

Tom Wolfe (right) autographs one of his books for Debbie and Champlin Sheridan.

More than 1,400 people celebrated the 25th anniversary of the Milton S. Eisenhower Library on April 20, 1990, at a special convocation held in Shriver Hall during which the renowned author Tom Wolfe was given the honorary degree of doctor of humane letters. After words of welcome to a standing-room-only audience, George Radcliffe, chairman of the board of trustees, recalled the day 25 years ago when former University President Milton S. Eisenhower opened the library named for him. Radcliffe extended a special welcome to John Eisenhower, nephew of Milton S. Eisenhower, and his wife Joanne, who were both in the audience. Scott Bennett, library director, followed with an impassioned speech about how the contents of libraries stir our imaginations and provide places "where we discover what we did not know before." "No other single place—no other building—expresses so fully," Bennett said, "the community of experience and purpose that we seek and still can find in higher education."

Shale Stiller, University trustee and chairman of the Library Advisory Council, expressed gratitude to the many people who support the library and who have brought us to the halfway point in raising the $4 million needed to match the NEH challenge of $1 million for the humanities collections of the library. As examples of this generosity, Stiller recognized two donations: those of the classes of 1939 and 1990. Pointing to the two enlarged bookplates displayed on the stage, he explained

FIGURE 8-2 Vanderbilt University Friends' Newsletter

Published three times a year by
The Friends of the Library
The Jean and Alexander Heard Library
Vanderbilt University
Nashville, Tennessee

Volume 14, No. 2
Fall 1989

Writer Richard Marius to Speak at Friends' 16th Annual Dinner

Richard Marius, director of expository writing and senior lecturer at Harvard University, will address the 16th annual meeting of the Friends of the Library on Thursday evening, November 2, at the University Club.

In his talk, "Life Into Fiction," Marius will describe how a writer turns his life experiences into a novel. He will discuss his latest book, tentatively titled *Once in Arcadia*, which is set in Tennessee. The book is slated for publication in 1990.

A native of Lenoir City, Tennessee, Marius taught history for 14 years at the University of Tennessee before joining the Harvard faculty in 1978.

He is the author of several books, including a biography, *Thomas More* (1984); a biographical study, *Luther* (1974); novels, *Bound for the Promised Land* (1976) and *The Coming of Rain* (1969); and writing guides and handbooks, *A Short Guide to Writing About History* (1989), *A Writer's Companion* (1984), and *The McGraw-Hill English Handbook*, with Harvey Wiener (1984). Marius has also written numerous articles and reviews for journals, newspapers, and other publications, and he has lectured extensively about Thomas More and the Renaissance.

Marius consults frequently with high school and college students and administrators about writing and writing programs. He has been a consultant for the National Humanities Faculty and directs the Tennessee Governor's Academy for Writing at the University of Tennessee. His interests include writing and literature, music, baseball, travel, Southern culture, and "perhaps, above all, good talk."

Good talk will be a hallmark of the evening, which begins with cocktails at 6:30 followed

Richard Marius

by dinner at 7:30. The event is open only to current members of Friends, and tickets are $25 per person.

Professor Charles Delzell, president of the Friends, will report on the past year's activities during a short business session.

To make dinner reservations, renew membership in the Friends, or join for the first time, please call the Library Development office at 322-7102.

◆ 1 ◆

PUBLICATIONS

NEWSLETTER

Perhaps the single most important public relations tool is the newsletter. In it the university library can best express what it is trying to do, what it hopes to accomplish, and why support is essential, not only to the library but also to the university and the larger community. It is not uncommon for libraries to devote considerable time to producing a fine publication. It is often said that it takes about the same amount of time to produce a mediocre publication as it is does to produce a first-rate one. This being the case, use the time to produce the best one possible.

There is tremendous competition for our attention every day. Often, we have neither the time nor the interest to adequately read, or even glance at, all the publications we receive. Before you begin, spend some time examining other academic library newsletters to assess what you like and do not like, what is necessary and appropriate and what is not. All the time keep in mind what your objectives are for the newsletter, what you want your readers to know about your library, and what action will result from having read your newsletter.[6]

The first element is design. Design includes the layout, use of pictures, graphic elements (including logos), and size. The design is critical because it will create a mood, a feeling about the content. It will evoke an emotion. Your goal is to design a newsletter that compels the reader to take the first step—to look at the newsletter—the next step—actually read it—and the last step—react to your message in the way that you intended.

Strive for harmony in the typeface, margins, headers, and illustrations. Margins should be liberal, providing contrast between the text and the page. You should also include a balanced mixture of illustrations and text. Good photographs often tell your story more effectively than words. A rule of thumb is to have about one picture for each page of your newsletter. However, to enhance design, you may have two (or more) pictures on one page and none on the next.

Photographs should always be of the highest quality. Nothing looks worse than a poor photograph in a publication. It sends the message that you care so little for the enterprise that you allow anything to be included. The reader will quickly lose interest. Find a photographer who does high quality work. Strive for a mix of posed and candid shots. Often it is necessary to pose a picture to include key people. However, you can also achieve better results by patiently waiting for the right shot.

Be sure to consider the graphic elements and logos used in the publication. It is important to maintain a look consistent with other university publications. Your reader needs to recognize immediately that this piece comes from an organization they know. The effect can be achieved in a number of ways. Use of the university seal or logo somewhere in the publication is appropriate. Washington University in St. Louis has a very attractive logo that incorporates the seal. Their friends newsletter includes this logo as part of the return address to let readers see that the newsletter is from the library and also from the university. Another way to achieve visual unity is to coordinate the color scheme for your publications with the university's print materials. Fundamentally, you must send a clear, consistent message that people will easily recognize and remember.

If you are considering changing the appearance of a publication, do not do so without seeking creative advice and professional consultation. There are several steps to consider. First, you need approval to make changes. Second, assemble a committee to represent different campus segments. Third, examine your identity. You cannot make a change until you have a firm grasp of who you are. Fourth, analyze your competition. Look at materials from other successful programs and borrow liberally from them. Finally, design your look and stick with it. Your design should be one that you want to live with for a long time.[7]

Another consideration is length and content of the newsletter. While this will vary depending upon how much information you want to convey in each issue, the newsletter should be between four and eight pages to provide adequate coverage.

The newsletter content should highlight people, especially your donors. It is no secret that people like to read about themselves and, in this context, how they have had an impact on the library. Specific articles should focus on how their contributions (money, collections, service, etc.) have made a significant difference to the university library. Donor recognition is essential. Not only does it honor and recognize the help of your donors, but it sends a message to others that they too can help the cause with their contributions. Often people want to help but are not sure how. Show them in your publications.

In each issue, include an "opportunity to join" section. This can be a form that lists various giving levels, a place for name and address information, and a brief description of membership benefits. The form has two purposes. First, you want the newsletter to be seen by many nonmembers, and the form is an easy way for the reader to become a member. Second, having this form in each issue sends a signal to your membership that the organization acknowledges the importance of its membership and wants to provide anyone who reads the newsletter every opportunity to join.

Next consider frequency. How often should this publication be mailed for maximum effect? The answer may be determined by factors beyond your control, such as budget limitations. Ideally, it should be determined by how active the organization is and by what you are trying to achieve with the newsletter. For an Association of Research Libraries (ARL) institution, friends groups should be active enough to produce at least two newsletters annually, and three if possible (issues being mailed in the fall, winter, and spring). Some friends groups are active enough to produce a quarterly newsletter. As long as the quality of the publication remains high, you should get your message out as frequently as you can.

Finally, who is the audience for your newsletter? Your first concern is for your members—those who are actually making gifts to the library. In addition, there are hosts of constituencies that should be informed of library activities: the university Board of Trustees, the directors of the Alumni Association, faculty and senior administrative staff, university librarians, staff from the university alumni and development operation, and retired faculty and librarians. If you are with a state institution you may want to include state agencies and key legislators. These groups, and others, have an interest in the library and are potential donors.

ALUMNI MAILINGS

Careful planning should be done at the time you decide whether or not to do an alumni mailing to attract new members. Do you want to go to the expense of an all-alumni mailing, or would it be more practical to segment the alumni mailing list? You can segment alumni by degree(s) received, date of attendance, major subject, and location.

ALUMNI MAGAZINES

In addition to newsletters and mailings, university-wide publications offer you the opportunity to get your message before the readers. Alumni magazines inform alumni and friends about the institution, often in an attractive magazine format that is usually published quarterly. It is advisable to use these publications sparingly for coverage of major events. For example, in December 1991 Vanderbilt University will celebrate the 50th anniversary of the establishment of the Joint University Libraries. Although this library system, one of the first cooperative systems, is no longer in place, it will be an opportunity to recognize the library as an integral part of the university. Plans include an article on the history of the library, its origins, the formation of the joint university library concept, and its eventual restructure. This article will fit well in an overall public relations strategy: to communicate to alumni and friends those issues which focus attention on the university library.

NEWS RELEASES

News releases should also be part of your public relations strategy. Depending on the type of event or activity you are attempting to publicize, the news release can be an effective way to tell the larger community. In terms of writing style, clear and concise language produce the most favorable results. It should be clearly identified as a news release—typed, double spaced, and with the name of the person to contact for additional information. Most universities have a sophisticated institutional relations program to assist you with the production and dissemination of news releases.

MEDIA CONTACTS

One way to increase the chances of your release being printed is to establish personal contact with people in the media. Let them know that you appreciate their support and that you are always available to assist them in covering your library events. Getting acquainted with local reporters will help ensure success for your public relations efforts.

SUMMARY

This overview of public relations programs to support development in academic libraries is by no means exhaustive. It is, rather, illustrative of some key factors to assist you as you reflect on what you are currently doing in these areas or on how you might get started.

Here then is a review of key points from the chapter. First, goals and objectives should be specific. They should be quantifiable to measure the success of whatever you are trying to achieve. They should be yearly, as well as quarterly, set far enough ahead to allow for adequate preparation time.

Second, staffing plays a key role in the effectiveness of your public relations effort. The development officer in an academic research library may also be responsible for public relations. A good working relationship with the university's public relations organization should be a priority. There are certain skills necessary for public relations officers: excellent written and verbal communications skills, flexibility, the ability to concentrate on several projects simultaneously, and, above all, a complete commitment to and belief in what you are doing. Your attitude will influence the behavior of others. Affiliation with professional organizations will give you opportunities to learn new skills.

Third, use a variety of media to support what you intend to accomplish. A combination of newsletter, alumni magazine, brochure, newspaper (both local and campus), as well as radio and television can help in your attempt to enlist support.

Fourth, the most effective public relations tool is the library newsletter. It is the library's best opportunity to get its message to donors and potential donors. It should be of the highest quality, not in terms of cost, but in terms of attention paid to detail.

The newsletter should be carefully designed. The elements of layout, photographs, graphic elements such as logos, and length should be well thought out and determined by the objectives you have set for this publication. You should strive to work in conjunction with your university publications office to gain a consistency of appearance while at the same time offering your readers something distinctive. The newsletter should focus on people. People enjoy reading about others with similar interests. It will be an effective way to influence your readers by showing how important their support can be and how it will be recognized.

Fifth, other publications can serve a public relations function for the library. These include alumni magazines, which reach a much larger audience. Care should be taken in determining what coverage to request. These publications come out quarterly, sometimes less often, and this infrequency will cause the editor to look carefully at the requests for coverage. Plan ahead and focus on a major event that could be the most useful in reaching a larger audience.

Sixth, news releases should also be part of your public relations strategy to reach the larger community. Use clear and concise language to get your message across. Work with your university relations office and establish a relationship of trust with the local media.

CONCLUSIONS

I am reminded of two stories that illustrate the work of a development/public relations officer in a large academic library. The first concerns noted architect Sir Christopher Wren. One day, as he was overseeing the reconstruction of St. Paul's Cathedral in London, he encountered two stonecutters and asked them what they were doing. The first replied, "I am cutting stone." The seconded responded by saying, "I am building a cathedral." It strikes me that this man's ability to see the "big picture" and understand that he is a part of something important will enable him to both enjoy his work and be the most productive. The same is true for each of us in our work. It forces us to come out from behind the narrow interests of our department and see that what we are doing affects the entire university community.

The second story involves a conversation I had with a colleague several years ago. At the time of this conversation he was the director of a large public university library and I was the director of a very small college library. One day as we rode to a meeting together he asked me how things were going at my library. I felt very inadequate talking with someone who seemed to have everything going for him. Finally, after I had rattled on for a few minutes, he said, "Yes, but are you doing what you ought to be doing?" In that one question he cut through to what was really important. No matter what size shop you have or what your resources are, there are certain things you can do to have a positive impact on those you are seeking to serve.

These two stories capture the essence of development/public relations work. We will be most successful if we can focus on the "big picture," distinguish those things that are important from those that are not, and concentrate on the former.

ENDNOTES

1. Jon Eldredge, "Internal Public Relations for the Academic Library," in *Persuasive Public Relations for Libraries,* (Chicago: American Library Association, 1983): 60.
2. Sue Fontaine, "The Role of Public Relations in Fund Raising," in *Library Development: A Future Imperative,* "Journal of Library Administration," 12, 4. Dwight F. Burlingame, ed. (Binghamton, NY, The Haworth Press, 1990): 17.
3. John E. Dolbois, "Public Relations," in *The International Encyclopedia of Higher Education,* 7, Asa S. Knowles, ed. (San Francisco, Josey-Bass, 1977): 3414.
4. Leo E. Geier, "Public Relations as an Arm of Development," in *Handbook of Educational Fund Raising,* Francis C. Pray, ed. (San Francisco, Josey-Bass, 1981): 205.
5. Fontaine, 17.
6. William R. Holman, "Library Friends Publications," in *Organizing the Library's Support,* D. W. Krummel, ed. (Urbana-Champaign, University of Illinois Graduate School of Library Science, 1979): 103.
7. Robert J. Rytter, "Of Logos and Letterheads," *Currents,* XIII, 7 (July/August 1987): 18.

9 DEVELOPMENT PERSONNEL

by Eileen M. Mulhare

If your goal in hiring a development officer is to delegate all responsibility for raising external funds, you will be disappointed with the outcome. As Berendt and Taft state bluntly, "development officers . . . do not, by and large, raise money" (1984:33).

Like a symphony conductor, the development officer orchestrates the effort but does not "make the music." It is the library's key leaders—the library director, library management team, trustees, faculty advisory board and committed volunteers—who raise funds by working in cooperation with the development officer. Where appropriate, development officers do write grant proposals and personally solicit prospects for gifts. Asking for money, however, is only one stage in a far more complex process involving prospect research, cultivation, solicitation and recognition.

What exactly do development officers do for academic libraries? In the simplest terms, they market the library as a cause worth supporting. Among the many functions they carry out are:

Planning and Goal Setting: Assisting the library leadership in setting annual goals, objectives and timetables for raising external funds.

Gifts Policies: Assisting the library leadership in establishing gift acceptance policies, for example, for endowed book funds or gifts-in-kind.

Prospect Research: Identifying and profiling potential sources of gift and grant support.

Prospect Clearance: Coordinating authorization to solicit, and approval of solicitation method, for approaching specific prospects.

Prospect Tracking: Developing and managing systems to track progress in solicitations.

Volunteer Management: Recruiting, training, motivating and coordinating volunteer leadership.

Donor Communications: Educating various constituencies about the library's needs through mission statements, case statements, brochures and other materials.

Annual Giving and Membership: Coordinating Friends of the Library programs and other strategies (direct mail appeals, phonathons) to solicit annual gifts.

Major Donors: Identifying and cultivating persons of wealth whose interests coincide with those of the library.

Corporate and Foundation Relations: Initiating and cultivating corporate and foundation contacts.

Grants and Other Major Funding: Coordinating grant applications, proposals, and other strategies to obtain funding for capital and other projects.

Planned Giving: Developing programs to obtain gifts through wills, bequests, stock transfers, and other prearranged methods.

Stewardship: Supervising acknowledgment, recording and recognition of gifts received, including annual giving reports, donor honor rolls and recognition programs.

(Adapted from Grasty and Sheinkopf 1982:9-10)

At some academic libraries, the development officer is responsible for "institutional advancement" or "external relations" functions. These activities involve overall public relations strategy and preparation of news releases, press information kits, annual reports, and other publications. The development officer may plan and promote a regular calendar of special events to involve donors, library users, and the general public in the life of the library.

STAFF COOPERATION

There is no general agreement on how to divvy up the labor between the development officer and other members of the library management team, particularly the librarians. It is clear that the typical development officer is overburdened with duties, priorities, and deadlines. What is impossible for one professional to accomplish alone, however, becomes possible with the help of gifted amateurs.

The gifted amateurs in this case are the librarians and other staff who routinely come in contact with potential donors. Their inter-action with faculty, alumni, corporate users, and other library constituencies can help set the stage for successful donor appeals and grant applications. In truth, the fund development program cannot advance without cooperation from the librarians.

The librarians' advice is crucial to setting realistic fundraising goals, deciding acceptance policies for gift collections, and finding the proper wording for appeal letters or case statements. The development officer relies on librarians to supply vital intelligence on possible sources of gift and grant support. Librarians are often the most spokespeople to explain the library's needs to potential donors, particularly when making grant proposals. The success of the library's friends program depends greatly on the ingenuity and leadership of librarians. They play a central role in nurturing donors and volunteers. A personal thank you from the right librarian may mean more to the giver than an equally sincere acknowledgment letter from the library director.

It can be counterproductive to dictate what the role of librarians and other library staff ought to be in the fundraising process. Whatever approach is taken, it should give librarians:

- A major stake in the outcome
- The freedom to be creative in defining their role, and
- Recognition for their fundraising activities

One means of accomplishing this is to form an external funding committee composed of key librarians and chaired by the develop-ment officer. The committee, rather than the development officer, should be accountable for meeting the library's annual fundraising targets.

DEVELOPMENT PERSONNEL NEEDS

No one person can possibly cover every development function alone, nor does every academic library need to handle all these areas in-house. A review of the thirteen development functions listed earlier is a helpful first step in determining the library's development personnel needs. Which of these functions are being handled on behalf of the library by other administrative units in the college or university? Which services are unavailable or unsatisfactory? Which functions are being managed by existing units within the library, such as the public information officer, friends coordinator, gifts librarian or special programs librarian? The new development officer's duties should be designed to complement rather than duplicate the services and resources presently available within the library and the institution.

The library director should be thoroughly familiar with the services rendered (or potentially available) through the college or university's central development, alumni relations, and public relations offices. Central offices may offer expert advice and management for annual giving, alumni outreach, prospect research, media relations, events planning, or other critical functions. If the parent institution can provide substantial services of this type, the library may only need a development person of its own on a parttime basis. If centralized services are weak and the library must create a comprehensive fundraising program virtually from scratch, the new development position will necessarily be full-time.

Some library staff are probably engaged in institutional advancement activities already, such as events, publications, donor recognition or friends programs. The library director should be well-versed in the state of the library's own external relations efforts. The question then becomes whether the new development officer will take over supervision of some or all of these functions, in addition to strictly fundraising duties, or will serve instead as an advisor to the staff assigned to these areas.

If the library's external relations activities are disorganized, understaffed or nonexistent, the library director may want to hire other personnel before recruiting a development officer. The success of the library's fundraising plans will depend not only on the creativity of the new development person but also on quality publications and news releases, a solid friends program and similar public outreach services.

FORECASTING

The final step in assessing development personnel needs involves an exercise in forecasting. What will the comprehensive fundraising agenda be for the library over the next three to five years? Among the issues that must be addressed are:

- Does the library need to establish or change its image with its constituencies (faculty, alumni, other users, and the public) before starting or expanding its fundraising programs?

- Will the library undertake any major construction, renovation, or endowment projects in the foreseeable future?
- Is the college or university planning to include the library in an upcoming capital campaign?
- Has the library annual giving program reached its potential or can it be strengthened or expanded?
- Has the library reached its potential in attracting support from persons of wealth, corporations, and foundations or do these areas need more attention?
- Will the library need major grants to accomplish its institutional goals?
- Will the library seek donations of significant private collections?

Each of these questions implies a different though related set of skills. The answers will suggest what specific strengths the library should seek in hiring a development professional and whether more than one new hire will be needed to implement the fundraising agenda.

THE JOB DESCRIPTION

The following brief job description is based on a hypothetical library's internal and institutional development resources, future fundraising plans, and the specific skills sought in a development officer:

> The University Library System invites applications for the newly created position of Director of Development. The position reports to the University Librarian and is responsible for:
>
> 1. Planning and implementing all major gifts efforts involving individuals, corporations, and foundations in preparation for a universitywide capital campaign
> 2. Interfacing with the university's Annual Giving Office in planning direct mail and phonathon appeals, primarily to alumni
> 3. Chairing the Library External Funding Committee and

4. Coordinating the Library System's overall fundraising programs.

The position supervises a full-time secretary and part-time student assistant, and is required to cooperate closely with the Library System's public information officer, gifts librarian, and Library Friends coordinator. The Director of Development serves as the primary link between the Library System and potential funding sources. The position represents the Library System with all other university offices involved in external relations.

QUALIFICATIONS

To serve effectively as a member of the academic library management team, the development officer requires at least a college education and some familiarity with fundraising in a higher education setting. A standard list of qualifications might include: a bachelor's degree with a minimum of three years' experience in fundraising for higher education; advanced degree and/or library experience preferred; evidence of progressive career achievements and continuing professional development; excellent written and oral communications skills; demonstrable competence in public relations; ability to design and implement programs; strong leadership skills and resultsoriented management style combined with good interpersonal skills.

The question is often asked, who is best qualified for a library fund development position, the library professional familiar with fundraising techniques or the development professional acquainted with library operations? In fact, library directors find good candidates in either pool. When surveyed recently, about one-third of the members of Development Officers of Research Academic Libraries (DORAL) identified themselves as present or former librarians. The other two-thirds reported fund development as their primary profession.

The library director should not hesitate to consider an otherwise qualified candidate who has no background in libraries and information science. The true development professional is by definition a "quick study." Most expect to serve more than one type of organization in the course of their careers. As Brakeley (1980:89) points out, the competent development officer seeks to establish rapport quickly with all the institution's constituencies. This includes learning their language and concerns, as well as mastering the technical terms to speak persuasively about the institution's mission and needs.

A librarian with little fundraising experience can lead a development program successfully if he or she has the right aptitude and is willing to seek the necessary training. Grasty and Sheinkopf (1982:6) offer the reassuring suggestion that "... most of the (institutional advancement) skills can be learned. Good common sense and character traits cannot." Berendt and Taft (1984:35) conclude that an inordinately "quiet, dull or inarticulate" person will have trouble in the fund development field no matter how much related training he or she receives.

Regardless of the candidate's prior background, some personality characteristics seem essential for success as a development officer: the ability to inspire, persuade, and motivate others; an exceptional level of personal honesty, integrity, idealism, compassion, and tolerance; creativity, perseverance, and the willingness to work hard; the capacity to handle failure without getting discouraged; and a talent for adapting readily to new people and circumstances (Berendt and Taft 1984:34; Brakeley 1980:7,63; Broce 1986:4142; Grasty and Sheinkopf 1982:5).

SALARY AND TITLE

Recruiting and retaining such a paragon demands an appropriate salary. The development officer's contribution to the bottom line makes it obvious how much he or she is worth, not only to the library but to rival institutions competing for scarce talent. Higher education fundraisers are among the highest paid in the development profession. The adage "you get what you pay for" most certainly applies.

Precise salary scales cannot be presented here but some guidelines are worth mentioning. Offer a salary commensurate with the candidate's educational attainment and experience. Compensation should be consistent with what comparable members of the library's management team are earning. Anything less invites the new hire to move elsewhere within a few years. Do not propose compensation based on a percentage of funds raised, that is, contingency fees or commissions. While not illegal, commission fundraising is considered highly unethical by members of the profession. No legitimate development specialist will agree to such an arrangement. Further guidance is available by consulting the salary surveys published periodically by the Council for the Advancement and Support of Education and the National Society of Fund Raising Executives.

The new development position also requires a suitable title. Director of Development, a popular and straightforward label, may be confused with library collections development. Preferable alternatives are Director of Fund Development, Resource Development, or Library Advancement. If the new hire will discharge other functions as well, specify them in the title. Customary add-ons are Community or Public Relations, Community or Public Affairs, Marketing, Grants and Sponsored Research, or Sponsored Programs. (For commonly used titles, see Mulhare and Wright 1988:2,8). Where personnel policies prevent the use of the term director, Development Manager, Officer, or Associate may be acceptable. Whatever the title selected, it should portray the officer to the public, the library staff, and the academic community as a member of the library's upper management.

RECRUITMENT STRATEGIES

Where does the library director find qualified candidates for the development post? Not by advertising in the local newspaper, unfortunately. Such an ad can net hundreds of applicants but few if any qualified candidates.

The library can reach a national audience of experienced fundraisers by advertising in The Chronicle of Higher Education, The Chronicle of Philanthropy, The Non Profit Times and The NSFRE News (National Society of Fund Raising Executives). Advertising opportunities closer to home vary from region to region. The institution's central development office may know of publications aimed at the local nonprofit community or newsletters published by local associations of development professionals.

A number of placement services specialize in fundraising personnel for nonprofits. The National Society of Fund Raising Executives operates an employment service as do many of the society's's local chapters. Among the better known executive recruiters in the field are Brakeley Recruiting (New Canaan, CT), Ketchum, Inc. (Pittsburgh, PA), Kittelman & Associates (Chicago,IL), and Snelling, Kolb & Kuhnle (Washington, DC).

Word-of-mouth in the local nonprofit community may be the best way to attract qualified applicants. Colleges and universities routinely recruit development personnel from other charitable and educational institutions, consulting firms, foundations, and the for-profit professions of communications, journalism, advertising, and public relations (Mulhare and Wright 1988: 2,6; Brakeley 1980:55).

When reviewing an applicant's resume, the library director should not be surprised to see a job change every two-to-five years. Seasoned professionals and even talented newcomers are in strong demand. Raiding staff from other organizations is a common, albeit unfortunate, practice. Most nonprofits offer fundraisers few opportunities for internal promotion, which adds to the turnover problem (Mulhare and Wright 1988:2,15). The lesson for the library is to offer a competitive salary and possibilities for career advancement. For example, a valued development officer could eventually be asked to head all public affairs or marketing functions.

Some experts recommend hiring a fundraising consultant on a temporary basis to analyze personnel needs, draft the job description, conduct initial interviews and check references (Berendt and Taft 1984:39; Brakeley 1980:58). This approach can help the library avoid a costly mistake, particularly if no one in-house has experience evaluating development staff.

PROFESSIONAL SOCIETIES AND CONTINUING EDUCATION

Few applicants for development jobs are likely to have college-based preparation for fundraising careers. Only a handful of accredited institutions award graduate or undergraduate degrees in fundraising administration. A few others grant certificates. Since 1982, about 20 academic centers for the study of philanthropy and voluntarism have opened around the country (Hodgkinson 1988). The mission of these mostly post-baccalaureate programs is to train researchers and policymakers rather than fundraisers.

As a result, the majority of development specialists acquire their skills on the job and by participating in continuing education programs sponsored by professional societies. Eight such organizations are listed in Appendix A.

The two primary affiliations for fundraisers in higher education are the National Society of Fund Raising Executives and the Council for the Advancement and Support of Education. Independent Sector and the American Association of Fund Raising Counsel serve as major information clearinghouses on charitable giving and voluntarism. Specific training and publications for library specialists are available through the Association of College and Research Libraries, the Library Administration and Management Association, Friends of Libraries U.S.A. and the Association of Research Libraries.

The National Society of Fund Raising Executives (NSFRE), founded in 1960, has over 11,000 members in more than 100 chapters throughout the United States. It is the only broad-based association serving individuals in the profession rather than institutions. Benefits include a monthly newsletter, quarterly magazine, and access to an exceptionally active network of local chapters.

NSFRE

The National Society of Fund Raising Executives (NSFRE), founded in 1960, has over 11,000 members in more than 100 chapters throughout the United States. It is the only broad-based association serving individuals in the profession rather than institutions. Benefits include a monthly newsletter, quarterly magazine, and access to an exceptionally active network of local chapters.

NSFRE sponsors an annual International Conference and several formal educational programs:

- First Course in Fund Raising (two days)
- Survey Course on Fund Raising Fundamentals (two days)
- Executive Leadership Institute (three days) and
- The CFRE examination leading to the status of Certified Fund Raising Executive

NSFRE courses are presented in more than 20 cities yearly. In addition, each local NSFRE chapter organizes its own annual conference, a schedule of monthly luncheon programs and other activities.

CASE

The Council for the Advancement and Support of Education (CASE) was formed in 1974 through the merger of the American Alumni Council (established in 1913) and the American College Public Relations Association (established in 1917). CASE's interests encompass not only fundraising but also alumni administration, public relations, marketing, and student recruitment. Membership is comprised of accredited institutions. About 3,200 colleges, universities, and independent schools belong. Individuals participate as institutional representatives. The number of representatives allotted to each member institution is based on student enrollment.

The parent institutions of most academic libraries are CASE members. For a modest annual fee, the library can ask to have its development officer added to the roster of CASE institutional representatives. Benefits include a subscription to the monthly magazine, reduced fees for educational programs, and discounts on CASE's extensive list of how-to books and pamphlets. CASE presents more than 50 different conferences and workshops throughout the country each year. Rounding out the schedule is a national meeting and separate annual conferences for each of CASE's eight regional divisions.

IS

Independent Sector (IS) is a consortium of 650 nonprofits, corporations, and foundations dedicated to promoting charitable giving and voluntarism. It is best known for its public awareness campaigns and scholarly research initiatives. The IS publication series covers a wide range of subjects, from management guides and national surveys to the writings of noted philanthropists. Individuals can join IS as associate members. Benefits includes a newsletter, discounts on publications, and notices of federal, state, and local legislative actions likely to affect the nonprofit community.

AAFRC

The American Association of Fund Raising Counsel (AAFRC), founded in 1935, is comprised of the nation's leading consulting firms. Its Fair Practice Code not only sets standards for consultants but serves as an excellent introduction to the ethical issues facing all fundraising professionals. AAFRC is recognized for its leadership in sponsoring philanthropy research. Among its regular publications is the statistical annual, Giving USA, a key reference volume on trends in charitable giving.

ACRL

The Association of College and Research Libraries (ACRL) of the American Library Association periodically publishes articles on fundraising strategies in its magazine, College and Research Libraries. ACRL's Task Force on Sources of Revenue in Academic Libraries hosts preconference sessions and discussion groups in conjunction with gatherings of the American Library Association and at ACRL meetings. The Task Force also works on documenting external funding patterns among academic libraries.

LAMA

The Fund Raising and Financial Development Section of the Library Administration and Management Association (FRFDS-LAMA) hosts a number of programs at the summer and midwinter conferences of the American Library Association. FRFDS-LAMA organizes formal presentations on fundraising topics, recruits consultants to act as table hosts, and fields a discussion group for development officers. A popular service is the Fund Fare Exchange, featuring take-home samples of brochures, appeal letters, and other materials contributed by FRFDS-LAMA members. FRFDS-LAMA activities and publications serve as the principal clearinghouse for information on library fundraising.

FOLUSA

Friends of Libraries U.S.A. (FOLUSA) is the foremost source of information and ideas for library membership programs. In its guide books and newsletter, FOLUSA shares examples of proven techniques for successful recruitment, renewal, recognition, events planning, and media relations. FOLUSA's principal meetings occur at conferences of the American Library Association.

ARL-OMS

The Office of Management Studies of the Association of Research Libraries (ARL-OMS) has published two SPEC Kits on library fund development. Especially useful are the samples of appeal letters, brochures, task assignments, and other materials submitted by ARL members.

For addresses and phone numbers of the eight professional organizations discussed here, see Appendix A.

REFERENCES

Berendt, Robert J. and J. Richard Taft. *How to Rate Your Development Office: A Fund Raising Primer for the Chief Executive.* Washington, DC: ___. Taft Corporation, 1984.

Brakeley, George, Jr. *Tested Ways to Successful Fund Raising.* New York, NY: AMACOM, 1980.

Broce, Thomas E. *Fund Raising: The Guide to Raising Money from Private Resources.* 2nd Ed. Norman: University of Oklahoma Press, 1986.

Grasty, William K. and Kenneth G. Sheinkopf. *Successful Fundraising: A Handbook of Proven Strategies and Techniques.* New York: Charles Scribner's Sons, 1982.

Hodgkinson, Virginia A. *Academic Centers and Research Institutes Focusing on the Study of Philanthropy, Volunteerism and Not-for-Profit Activity: A Progress Report.* Washington, DC: Independent Sector. November 1988.

Mulhare, Eileen M. and Sandra E. Wright. *Compensation and Other Characteristics of Michigan Fund Raising Professionals. Results of the 1987 Membership Survey, Michigan Chapter—National Society of Fund Raising Executives.* Monograph. NSFRE-Michigan: Dearborn, 1988.

APPENDIX A

PROFESSIONAL SOCIETIES FUNDRAISING AND PHILANTHROPY

American Association of Fund Raising Counsel
25 West 43 Street
New York, NY 10036
(212) 354-5799

Council for the Advancement
and Support of Education
11 Dupont Circle, Suite 400
Washington, DC 20036
(202) 328-5900

Independent Sector
1828 L Street, N.W.
Washington, DC 20036
(202) 223-8100

National Society of Fund Raising Executives
1101 King Street, Suite 3000
Alexandria, VA 22314
(703) 684-0410

CONTINUING EDUCATION LIBRARY-RELATED PROGRAMS

To reach the Association of College and Research Libraries (Task Force on Sources of Revenue in Academic Libraries), the Library Administration and Management Association (Fund Raising and Financial Development Section), and Friends of Libraries U.S.A., contact:

American Library Association
50 East Huron Street
Chicago, IL 60611
(312) 944-6780

To obtain information on SPEC Kits for academic library fundraising, contact:

Association of Research Libraries
Office of Management Studies
1527 New Hampshire Ave., N.W.
Washington, DC 20036
(202) 232-2466

CONTRIBUTORS

Charlene Clark is the Development and Promotions Coordinator for the Texas A&M Sterling C. Evans Library. She has a doctoral degree in English from Louisiana State University. She has also worked for a number of years in institutional public relations and has taught English and literature courses. Active in the American Library Association she has written widely on library development issues.

Barbara I. Dewey is Director of Administrative and Access Services at The University of Iowa Libraries, where she has, in addition to other duties, responsibility for development and public relations. She holds bachelor's and master's degrees from the University of Minnesota and has held positions in a number of academic libraries including Northwestern University and Indiana University.

Joan M. Hood is Director of Development and Public Affairs for the University of Illinois Library System at Urbana-Champaign. She is an incorporator, past president, and Distinguished Board Member of Friends of Libraries U.S.A., and past president of the Illinois Center for the Book. She has lectured widely on library development. During the past six years the Library's Development Office has raised more than $12 million in private support and qualified for a $1 million National Endowment for the Humanities Challenge Grant. She received her B.A. in French from the University of New Hampshire and also studied at the Universite Laval, Quebec City, and did graduate studies at Harvard University.

Susan P. Jordan has served as Director of Library Development at Northwestern University since 1984. For the previous ten years she worked in financial services in Chicago and San Francisco. She received the bachelor's degree from Dominican College in San Rafael, California and in 1990 received the Master of Management degree from Northwestern University's Executive Management Program.

Alison Wheeler Lahnston is Director of Major Gifts in the Faculty of Arts and Sciences at Harvard University. A graduate of Radcliffe College, she holds an M.S. in Library Science from Simmons College and an M.B.A. from George Washington University. She was formerly Director of Planned Giving at Wheaton College and Director of Planned Giving and Stewardship at Boston University.

William R. Mott is Director of Development, Jean and Alexander Heard Library, Vanderbilt University. A former junior college president, he received the B.A. degree in history from the University of Mississippi and the Ph.D. in higher education from Vanderbilt University. He has consulted at institutions of higher education on academic library development concerns.

Eileen M. Mulhare is currently Research Associate in the Department of Sociology and Anthropology at Colgate University, Hamilton, New York, and a fund development consultant to nonprofit organizations. She formerly served as Director of Grants and Development for the Wayne State University Library System in Detroit. An active participant in many professional fundraising organizations, she holds the Ph.D. degree in anthropology and economic development from the University of Pittsburgh.

Mary Bailey Pierce is Director of Development at the University of Miami, Coral Gables, Florida. Her primary responsibilities are in annual, capital, and planned giving for the College of Arts and Sciences and the University Libraries. Her professional background includes more than a decade of experience in the successful implementation of both annual and capital fundraising programs in independent higher education. She has also served as senior fundraising counsel to several national health and human services organizations.

Linda J. Safran is Associate Director of Resource Development for The Enterprise Foundation in Columbia, Maryland. Prior to that she was a development officer at Johns Hopkins University with responsibilities for hospital and the School of Medicine fundraising. She also served as Director of Library Development at the Milton S. Eisenhower Library where over $5,000,000 was raised in three years and a $1,000,000 National Endowment for the Humanities Challenge Grant was secured.

Helen Willa Samuels is the Massachusetts Institute of Technology Institute Archivist and Head, Special Collections. She has held positions at the University of Cincinnati and Radcliffe/Harvard University. She holds the M.L.S. degree from Simmons College and the bachelor's degree from Queens College. She is a Fellow of the Society of American Archivists and has written and received many grants.

Samuel A. Streit has been Assistant University Librarian for Special Collections at Brown University since 1977. He was responsible for a 1978 National Endowment for the Humanities Challenge

Grant that led to the renovation of the John Hay Library, a project that had as its centerpiece the preservation and conservation of the library's special collections. He has been involved with the Brown library's other preservation activities and has served on the Advisory Committee of the Northeast Document Conservation Center from 1978 to 1986.

INDEX